Night Letters

Inside

Wartime

Afghanistan

Books by Rob Schultheis

Fool's Gold: Lives, Loves, and Misadventures in the Four Corners Country

Bone Games: Extreme Sports, Shamanism, Zen, and the Search for Transcende

The Hidden West: Journeys in the American Outback

Night Letters: Inside Wartime Afghanistan

Night Letters

Inside
Wartime
Afghanistan

Rob Schultheis

THE LYONS PRESS
Guilford, Connecticut
An imprint of The Globe Pequot Press

For Nancy

The Lyons Press is an imprint of The Globe Pequot Press

Originally published in 1992 by Crown Publishers, Inc., New York.

First Lyons Press edition, 2001

2 4 6 8 10 9 7 5 3 1

Printed in Canada

The Library of Congress Cataloguing-in-Publication Data
is available on file.

Night Letters: An Introduction

2001: Back to Afghanistan

*B*ack in the innocent days of the Jihad, the Afghan war of liberation against the Soviet Empire, we used to talk about what peace would be like, when it came.

Journalists, aid workers, mujahedin fighters, and political officers sat around hotel rooms in Peshawar, chaikhannas in Khost, guerrilla camps in the snowy Safed Koh and Koh-i-Baba, dreaming of Afghanstan as Shangri-la, Paradise. The bombed-out villages would be rebuilt, the canals and karezes repaired, the fields green again, the orchards bloom, mosques and schools rise from the ashes. Elders and wise men (and women) would convene to unite the tribes in a new, free nation.

Most of us journalists were stringers, freelancers, war junkies, and romantics who had ricocheted into the Afghan war like shrapnel and ended up staying out of love for the country, the people, and their struggle. One whacked-out cameraman mused about owning a club in post-war Kabul, a sort of Central Asian Rick's with himself as Bogey, where old mujaheds, newsies, and Central Asian hands would gather to swig tea or puff a bong or sip an illicit vodka. A brave and pretty CNN reporter wanted to come back and found a string of women's schools across the countryside, combining Islamic studies with political empowerment, science, medicine, engineering: "Arming the women warriors of Afghanistan," she called it.

One enchanted evening in Peshawar, after a dusty, bloody trip into the war (bombs falling, villagers fleeing, kids sniping at MIGs with World War I Enfields), I sat in a garden with a French nurse and a group of young mujahedin intellectuals, and we invented a post-war Afghanistan National Park System, with me as chief. Watersheds, forests, and wildlife would be preserved, and all the money from tourism would go to local schools, agricultural projects, and clinics. "We have glaciers, we have Marco Polo sheep, we have monkeys, wolves, leopards," said one young guerrilla leader triumphantly. "Everyone in the world will want to come to Afghanistan!"

Sweet dreams, while the bombs fell and friends died and, looking back on it now, dreams destined to be killed.

In 1992, a few months before the mujahedin finally entered Kabul, a young Japanese photographer named Nako Nanjo was accompanying a guerrilla group near the Khyber Pass. A mujahed press flack asked her opinion of the war, how it was going. The Soviets had pulled the last of their troops out two years before, and the brutal puppet regime of ex–secret police chief Najibullah was steadily losing ground. The future looked as bright as the sunlight on the diamond peaks of the Safed Koh that day.

Nako thought for a moment, and then smiled. "Now the mujahedin are deciding their future," she said softly.

A few hours later, descending into the Kabul Gorge with a muj, column, she stepped a few inches off the trail, onto a Soviet antipersonnel mine hidden in the dust. A deafening explosion enveloped her body. She died a few minutes later, but not before she asked one of her companions to take a last portrait of her.

The photograph is almost unbearable to look at, even today: a frail broken girl sprawled on the stones, her pale face spattered with blood, black hair splayed like the plumage of a smashed bird.

Perhaps in a strange way she was lucky not to live to see what was to follow. It would have pained her, I think, more than that brief agony on the cruel slopes of the Kabul Gorge. Even today, I don't like to write about what became of the mujahedin "victory": how they won their war agaist all odds, and then lost everything. It is a sad, shameful story, and my own country, America, played such an ugly role in it all…. But the story should, must, be told.

The U.S. had an agreement with the Afghan resistance: After the war, when the Soviets were gone, we would help establish a stable, democratic government in Afghanistan, and aid in rebuilding the country. Back in the glory days of the British Empire, critics used to talk of "Perfidious Albion." Now, as the twentieth century segues into the twenty-first, it is "Faithless America." Ask the Hmong, the Kurds, the Tibetans, or any of the other peoples we persuaded to fight for us, waving our flag, our money and guns, and then promptly betrayed for a few pieces of silver.

"As long as the rivers run" . . . nothing has changed. Around the time the last Soviet-backed puppet fell in Kabul, the Cold War ended. Our priorities instantly changed, and faster than you can say "amoral" the United States government forgot all about Afghanistan: It was as if the place had never existed.

But there was worse. Just as we erased the last vestiges of Afghanistan from our conciousness, we invited our friends the Saudis and Pakistanis to set up shop in the ruins and squeeze the last drops of life from them.

This process had already begun during the Jihad, when the CIA allowed Pakistani military intelligence, ISI, to give most of our military aid to Pakistan's pet guerrilla leader, an unsavory character named Gulbuddin Heckmatyar. No matter that Gulbuddin had spent his pre-war years at Kabul University throwing acid in the faces of women students he dubbed "too liberated." Or that he was the prime suspect in the murders of several Western journalists, aid workers, and pro-Western Afghan intellectuals. Or that his troops spent more time fighting rival mujahedin groups than they did battling the Soviets. For years, the CIA sat blithely by as the Pakistanis armed this petty thug with the best and most of our weapons and money. Gulbuddin, for instance, was the first guerrilla leader to receive Stinger antiaircraft missiles, while his rival Achmad Shah Massood, the main architect of the Soviet defeat in Afghanistan, never received any. In one incident, ISI sent a booby-trapped truckload of ammunition to Massood that exploded on delivery and barely missed killing him. And still the CIA did nothing.

Why? I can think of reasons, but they are all unspeakably evil.

At the same time, the CIA was helping bring thousands of Arab volunteers unto Afghanistan to help fight the Soviets, though there was no evidence the Afghans needed more fighters, only better and more equipment and supplies. Like Gulbuddin, these religious Foreign Legionaires caused more trouble than they did good, murdering Afghan civilians they deemed "un-Islamic," harassing Western aid workers, and alienating the mujahedin they fought beside.

One of these Arabs, of course, was a wealthy young Yemeni-Saudi trust funder named Osama bin Laden, who, like many of his CIA-recruited Arab brethren, already despised the West and America in particular.

Again, Why? And again, I don't like the answers I come up with, not at all.

When the last Marxist regime collapsed and a Massood-led coalition took power in Kabul, the Pakistanis supplied Gulbuddin with thousands of missiles, that he rained down on the capital from the hills above. And meanwhile, Pakistanis and their Saudi masters readied another proxy force, in case Gulbuddin didn't pan out. In the refugee camps in Baluchistan, they were brainwashing thousands of war orphans, turning them into an army of fanatical drones, under the name "Taliban," or "religious students," ready to be loosed upon their own homeland.

To understand Taliban, one has to go back into the past, in Saudi Arabia. The current self-styled Saudi "royal family" are members of a fringe religious movement called Wahabism. Wahabis were marginal figures in Saudi Arabia, primitive hillbillies out of the mainstream of Saudi culture and society till they overthrew the aristocratic Mecca/Medina royal family after World War I. (The old Saudi royals, the ones who fought alongside Lawrence against the Turks, described themselves as "Neither Sunni nor Shi'a, just Moslems." They were tolerant, urban, urbane folks.)

The Wahabis are something quite the opposite. Founded by an eighteenth-century desert madman and cosmic scold named Abdul Wahab, Wahabism is mulishly atavistic, violently misogynistic, and viciously intolerant. Wahabis not only despise all non-Moslems, they despise their non-Wahabi fellow-Moslems just as much or more. Think of them as the Khmer Rouge of Islam. When they took over in Saudi Arabia, they immediately destroyed many of the country's oldest, finest mosques, on the grounds their beauty was somehow pagan. Art, music, literature, freedom, science— Wahabis hate them all, and dream of a world scourged of such evils and returned to an Ur-paradise as pure and dead as a pillar of salt.

Of course, like so many political puritans, they themselves live lives of personal corruption, venality, and hedonism so extreme as to verge on the surreal. The Saudi royals whore it in Europe, the U.S., and Thailand like a family of demented de Sades and gamble away millions in the world's most expensive casinos, all the while cursing the West that makes their existence possible and whose corruption they revel in. Which Saudi prince was it who beat his court dwarf to death in a Greek hotel lobby because he didn't like a joke the little man told, and had to be rescued from prison by the local CIA station chief? Little wonder they are beloved only by multinational oil companies and petro-politicians.

If you wonder about the cruel cynicism of these self-described saints, consider this: One of the main sources of funding for the Taliban/Wahabi machine in Afghanistan is the production and sale of opium and heroin. And where are 90 percent of these drugs sold? In Pakistan and Iran, where they have addicted millions of young Moslem kids. In Pakistan there are at least four million heroin addicts today. Every year, literally thousands of Iranian border guards are killed fighting armed heroin smugglers running the lethal tan dust from the heroin labs of Afghanistan into Iran to addict millions there. Moslem "mullahs" hooking their own kids on smack and riding around in silk shalwar kameezes in air-conditioned SUVs. Surely there is a special place in Jehannum, Hell, for these hypocrites.

Afghanistan was a perfect playpen for the Saudi royals. For one thing, they could send their most fanatical and criminally minded youths there as "holy warriors," ensuring that they didn't cause trouble at home.

And, just as important, they could use Afghanistan in their schemes of expansion and hegemonism.

For years the Saudis have been waging a kind of secret war inside the Islamic world, spreading the Wahabi creed by setting up fundamentalist madrassahs (religious schools) from Indonesia to Europe to North Africa to Africa, sponsoring terrorist groups, murdering moderate Sunni Moslems, Sufis, Shi'as, and any other followers of Islam with antiauthoritarian, progressive ideas. In Afghanistan, the Saudis and their Pakistani junior partners planned to set up what in essence was a Wahabi colonialist state, a base for further Wahabi expansionism and a bulwark against Saudi Arabia's great rival, Iran. As they carried out their de facto invasion of Afghanistan, beginning with the first Taliban cross-border offensive in 1995, the U.S. again sat by, smiling. Even when the Taliban and their ally (and money man) Osama bin Laden slaughtered tens of thousands of Afghan civilians in ethnic cleansing campaigns worse than the Serbian terror in Kossovo; even when bin Laden used Afghanistan as a base for terrorist attacks on American embassies, bases, and ships; even when Talibanization threatened to spread into Pakistan, in a classic case of intelligence "blowback," placing nuclear weapons in the hands of religious madmen.

Why? I hate to think.

As I continued to visit Afghanistan during the post-Jihad nineties, I got to see the Taliban's evils all too closely. I saw them, I reported on them—and no one listened. No one even wanted to listen. It was maddening, frustrating to the point of pitch black rage and despair. In the land of the blind the one-eyed man isn't king, he's cursed.

There I was in Taliban-ruled Kabul, for instance, visiting an orphanage, a cold concrete piss-stinking warehouse where hungry kids shivered and coughed on bare bunks or played outside in a vacant lot full of rubble and broken glass while Taliban mullahs as sleek as sea lions basked in the heat of the building's only stove in a cozy little office, eating sweets and sipping tea. The older female orphans were allowed outside just two hours every month, on the orphanage roof, to keep them from the temptations of the world. The rest of the time they were prisoners in that gloomy, frigid asylum, no books, no toys, no school, nothing....

Or in Mazar-i-Sharif, just before the Taliban takeover there, filming a refugee camp housing hundreds of educated Kabuli women and their children (husbands imprisoned or killed by Taliban). Their bright frightened faces, their wistful voices . . . To learn that when the Talibs took the city, all the women and children in the camp were massacred within a few hours (after the requisite rape, torture, etc.). And the laughing Hazara boy with the basket of roghini nan on his head in the bazaar, was he one of the thousands of his fellow-tribesmen who had their throats cut in the great mass execution ordered by Milosevician Mullah Nazian? Or was he one of the "fortunate" ones who merely had their right hands amputated for the crime of being (a) Shi'a, and (b) of Mongol ancestry? I filmed him too, and for a long time after I had nightmares that my dear little Sony minicam was somehow a deadly weapon, that slew everyone I met and loved and put on digital tape. Nightmares and, worse, daymares that came close to driving me crazy with guilt and sorrow, so sick-feeling I thought more than once about putting an end to myself.

Worst of all was Bamiyan Valley: Bamiyan of the great Buddhas, of the Silk Road chronicles, the Hazara heartland guarded by the 20,000 foot peaks of the Koh-i-Baba, Grandfather of the Snows. Bamiyan of the kindly Shi'a mullahs, the peasant women soldiers, the golden autumn trees . . . the most beautiful place on Earth I've ever been. Dead and gone now, its people slaughtered, the Buddhas themselves destroyed by tank and artillery fire and tons of high explosive. Wahabism in action . . . but I won't go there, not now, it's all too much. . . .

But as it turned out, I didn't have to go there. Now it's come here: September 11, 2001. Evil, leaping like lightning around the world.

As I write this, it's two weeks after the World Trade Center, the Pentagon, the 757s and 767s with their cargoes of doomed innocents. In another three weeks I'll be back in Afghanistan, *insh'Allah.* Some doctor friends and I have a little aid group called Refugee Relief International, or the Koh-i-Baba Group, depending on who you ask. The anti-Taliban Northern Alliance have asked—they want us to come over and organize clinics, medic training, and a transport system for the sick and wounded, civilians and fighters. The battle, the campaign, the Holy War is on, hot against the false prophets and the false-whiskered Infidels, for the poor, proud, and wise, God's lost tribes. It's autumn in the Hindu Kush now, in Badakshan and the Panjshir, and the snows will come soon. There's no time to lose—and there never should have been.

It's just like the old days: Jihad Time again. Now as then the fate of the world is being played out across those sky-scraping deserts, those bald, wrinkled badlands and razor-sharp mountains, tusks of snow, the dust of the saints . . . *Bismillah e rahman e raheem.*

In the Name of Allah the Most Merciful and Compassionate, this time we will not fail.

—Rob Schultheis
Telluride, Colorado
September 30, 2001

Prologue

ne winter, when the war was at its darkest and Afghanistan seemed lost, I
traveled across the Safed Koh Mountains with a mujahedin caravan. There were a
dozen armed guerrillas and about the same number of pack horses, loaded with sacks of flour, tins
of Kalashnikov ammunition, big recoilless rifle
rounds and olive-drab antitank mines, bound for
the resistance base at the bombed-out town of
Jegdeleg. We had crossed the border the night
before, to evade the MIGs and gunships that
hunted along the frontier. Now, like everyone else
on the trail, we trusted to luck, haste, and the
favor of Allah to survive.

Many people were traveling that day: thousands of us, toiling over the icy spine of those barren, dusty mountains. Bands of mujahedin like
ours and a few bold merchants and nomads trekked
north, toward the heart of the war zone. Hordes
of refugees, whole hemorrhaged villages and
towns, and armies of exhausted guerrillas passed

1

us, heading toward Pakistan and the bitter and unlasting peace of exile.

In the cold blue skies above, the enemy was busy, too. To the northwest, an Antonov spotter plane buzzed among the mountaintops, snooping for targets. Every few minutes there was a rumble of thunder, an earthquake in the heavens: we looked up and saw knife points of silver hurtling across the sky, south to north. As the MIGs vanished, another, deeper thunder would sound, the unmistakable voice of HE, high explosive. They were bombing the hell out of Tirzeen, west of Jegdeleg, trying to destroy the guerrillas who were based there, led by the legendary Commander Afghani.

All day long we had been hearing stories from the north, from southbound travelers, and all of them were bad. A Soviet armored and infantry column had attacked Jegdeleg a few days before and occupied the town briefly before pulling back; no one knew when they might return. A second, larger force was reportedly advancing on Tirzeen. Chopper-borne commandos had raided the trail up ahead several times in the last two weeks. One group had burned the teahouse in the hills beyond Azrow, and killed the popular proprietor. They doused the body with a chemical that rotted the flesh from the bones, disintegrated it, making a proper Islamic burial impossible. The storytellers were more outraged by this than anything else. It was a violation not only of man but, far worse, of man's ties with Allah: the ultimate kind of atrocity in Afghan eyes.

More jets dove down the vault of the sky above, more bombs grumbled and roared. Tirzeen was really taking it: they were bouncing the rubble around, turning the big pieces into little ones and the little pieces into dust. Men were dying there, I thought; and I felt a numb quid of fear in my throat that threatened to choke me. How could anyone, anything survive in that caldron of homicide, a fire which seemed to reach out for us and draw us into its heart?

As we reached the summit of the pass, climbing past snowdrifts and stands of wind-stunted drought-stricken timber, more MIGs screamed past overhead. The mujahedin had dug in heavy machine guns on the ridgelines beyond, and now they opened up at the jets, firing long rattling bursts. People on the trail cheered and yelled, but the muj may as well have been shooting at the moon. The MIGs were far out of range, and the antiaircraft gunners were hopelessly outmatched in firepower anyway. If the jets and helicopters came and attacked us here, we would be slaughtered. Back then in 1984, the Soviet empire cruised supreme in the skies over Afghanistan, killing with nonchalant ease.

We were descending the north side of the pass, scrambling down the steep rubble and frozen snowbanks. We passed another northbound pack train, a long column of horses and camels hauling a small arsenal of weaponry: bundles of rocket-propelled grenades, ammo cans, 12.7-mm machine guns, mortars and mortar shells. The animals were escorted by mujahedin and a group of gnarled old professional caravanners. Someone had given the old men plastic bags to wrap over their sandals, to keep the snow out, and they had discovered that the plastic made their feet fly on the steep snow. As we watched, a couple of them launched themselves down the mountainside, skidding, flailing their arms, whooping with glee.

Above, toward the far end of the caravan, another old man grinned, raised his long walking staff, and jammed it beneath the tail of the nearest camel. The beast reared, squawking and bellowing indignantly; its great hooves battered the next animal in line, stampeding the whole column, toppling men and animals like dominoes, sending them tumbling down the mountain. A camel lost its load, dozens of rockets flying through the snow; a pony bucked loose a shower of ammo cans. The old man who triggered the disaster leaned and rocked on his stick, laughing so hard that tears streamed down his wrinkled brown cheeks.

By some miracle no one, man or beast, was hurt, but the chaos was absolute. Bundles dangled from torn and tangled ropes. Horses neighed and camels hooted. Mujahedin lay upside down, assault rifles half buried in the snow, turbans unraveled on the slopes.

For a few moments the terrible old man laughed alone, but then one of the upended partisans joined in. The laughter jumped like wildfire down the wintry mountainside, and the victims of the trick laughed the loudest of all. It really was a beautiful joke, an Afghan classic, the kind the mountain people would talk about, sing about for years: "One time, during the Jihad, when the Shurovee [Soviets] were bombing, we crossed the mountains in the snow . . ."

His name sounded like "Marienbad," something like that, and when Robin and I came upon him he was making adobe bricks and stacking them in the middle of the canyon floor while two young men, his sons, stood guard over him with rifles. He was a middle-aged man, and clean shaven, which was strange for a rural Afghan, nut brown, beaming, with a balmy light in his eyes. His sons smiled proudly as he told us his story.

Back in 1976, long before anyone imagined the faintest chance of war, Marienbad had a dream. (He was one of the region's wealthiest merchants, with a reputation for both generosity and a certain ingenuous otherworldliness.) In his dream, he saw fire falling from the sky, great masses of it, falling onto the canyon, blasting the houses of the village to ruins, striking down his friends and neighbors. The dream shook him deeply; when he awoke the next morning, he immediately got a pick and shovel, went to the cliff behind his house, and began digging. When people asked him why, he told them about his vision: I am digging a shelter for the village, he said. He kept on working, for weeks, months; Marienbad's cave became a joke, from one end of the canyon country to the other.

Then, in 1978, the war came out of nowhere. The soldiers came from Kabul, with their Soviet advisers, their trucks and armor. The villagers barricaded the mouth of the canyon. There was fighting—muskets and swords, hunting rifles and homemade Molotov cocktails against artillery, grenades, machine guns. Somehow the villagers drove the invaders back. Two days later, the MIGs and helicopter gunships came, circling low over the rimrock. They began to fire rockets and cannons, drop bombs. The earthen houses of the village fell in torrents of deafening fire, but more than three hundred people fled to the safety of Marienbad's cave and were saved.

Now Marienbad had returned from the refugee camps in Pakistan, because of another dream. This one told him to return from exile to the ruined village and build a rest house along the trail for the mujahedin and refugees passing through. He was going to make the walls two feet thick, he said, with another stone wall around that, to protect against bomb blasts and shrapnel. Inside, there would be free tea and food for anyone who came. "When they hear about my rest house, the Shurovee will try to destroy it!" he smiled. "But the walls will be too strong!"

After a while, Marienbad led us to the wreckage of his house, nearby against the south wall of the gorge. It had been bombed and rocketed to pieces, but enough still remained that you could see how grand, how lovely it must have been: big sunny courtyards and rooms, fine carved woodwork on doors and balconies, stout roofbeams cut to last five hundred, a thousand years. A network of pipes beneath the floors had carried heat from the big bread ovens to the bedrooms, to warm them in winter. A cradle still hung in one of the blasted chambers, unutterably sad in that abandoned place.

Behind the house was the famous cave. It was bigger than I had expected, almost the size of a small ballroom, with a high ceiling and walls of smooth, chiseled stone. It looked like something out of "Aladdin's Lamp" or "Ali Baba," and it was almost impossible to visualize this one small, slender man excavating it by himself. I watched Marienbad looking at his handiwork, and in his eyes I could see the memory of the dream, the lonely labor, the mockery, and finally his beloved people taking shelter from the rain of steel and flame. He must have been touched by angels, the messengers of Allah.

▪ ▪ ▪

We were traveling with a band of teenage guerrillas from the ruined and subverted villages of the Nazian and Achin river valleys. The Soviets had bombarded most of these villages into debris and dust, and bribed, infiltrated, and blackmailed the rest into bitter submission. These were kids, really, but their eyes were ten thousand years old, and their smiles had a way of chilling out around the corners and fading away from you till they were as distant as the polar snows of Mars.

We had stopped in a *marcaz*, a guerrilla camp, on a desolate mountain. A battle was going on a few miles away: a Soviet convoy was trying to search out and destroy mujahedin bases in the area, and the resistance fighters had blocked its advance with a series of ambushes and hit-and-run raids. The Soviets were throwing in air power, MIGs, Sukhois, and helicopter gunships to try to break through.

We were sitting around the camp, drinking tea and talking, when word came in on the radio from the battlefield down-valley. The mujahedin had just shot down a MIG with a Stinger surface-to-air missile. The pilot had ejected and parachuted to safety, but when the Soviets sent a rescue chopper to pick him up, the guerrillas shot the helicopter down, too. The chopper crew was dead, but the MIG pilot had been captured at gunpoint and added to the dozen or so enemy airmen already held by the down-valley muj, who were among the first resistance fighters in Afghanistan to receive surface-to-air missiles, and who really knew how to use them.

One of our young guerrilla companions grinned wolfishly. "There are too many Shurovee prisoners at Tora Bora," he said. Tora Bora, or "Black Rock Mountain," was the stronghold of the down-valley partisans.

"We will have to get rid of them," one of the other kids said. "We can't afford to feed them anymore. Besides, the other Shurovee know they are there; sooner or later they will mount a commando operation to try and rescue them."

"We will have to kill them," another mujahed agreed, smiling happily. "We have no choice."

"What are you going to do?" I asked half seriously. "Shoot them?"

The bony kid who had spoken first burst into laughter, as if I had just told the funniest joke in the world. He had one of those infectious, irresistible laughs that pulls you in after it, and I found myself laughing, too. The other guerrillas were smiling, showing their teeth.

"Oh, no," the joker said, still laughing. "No shooting. Bullets are too *expensive*." The other muj were looking at each other, you could tell they had seen this routine before. "No shooting," the comedian repeated. "But"—and he went into a grotesque series of pantomimes: first a man having his throat cut, gurgling horribly, and then expiring; then picking up a handful of rocks and flinging them, one after another, zinging them with savage velocity, stoning an imaginary victim to death; and finally, pointing up the cliff and miming a man being thrown off, flailing his arms in bug-eyed terror, and smashing to pieces on the rocks . . .

You couldn't help but laugh (you *really* had to be there), even though you realized on one level that what the kid was acting out had a very good chance of coming true, flesh and blood, absolute reality, bitter and hilarious truth. In Afghanistan, it was boffo. These children with their hard, ancient eyes were the dragon's teeth of a war they had not chosen but had taken and made their own, and they laughed with a sense of unshakable righteousness that I could not deny. If you were not there, how could you ever understand?

one

It all begun by accident, really. I wasn't looking for Afghanistan; it just happened to be in the way. It was the summer of 1972, I was bound for India to work on a Ph.D. thesis in anthropology, and I decided to travel overland from Europe, partly to save money—it was cheaper than flying—and partly for adventure. The most direct route east from Turkey and Iran took you across the breadth of the country: Herat to Kandahar to Kabul, and on over the Khyber Pass to Pakistan.

The original name of the place, Yaghistan, means "Land of the Unruly," "Land of the Ungovernable," or "Land of the Out-of-Control," and you started hearing tales of its wildness long before you got there, from westbound travelers. There were a lot of them back then: all the borders were open, all the way to Kathmandu, and the road back and forth was crowded with young Westerners, hipsters, pilgrims, vagabonds. Everyone seemed to have a story about Afghanistan:

wacky tales of caravans, blind bards, wandering dervishes, horsemen, and gunfire in the night.

You came upon the country from Iran across an eerie, empty no-man's-land, a quarantine zone the Iranians had established to insulate themselves from poor, crazy Afghanistan. I was riding in a dilapidated minibus jammed with Westerners, border tribesmen, and Afghan merchants. Halfway across, the Afghan next to me jabbed my shoulder and pointed out into the wastelands, wobbly in the heat. I saw a line of camels, loaded with riders and goods, fading into the dust and haze. "Afghans," my companion said proudly. "Smuggler-man. Take *tariak* Iran. Much money—" He grinned. "Or maybe Iran, he shoot!" He laughed loudly.

"Tariak?"

"Tariak—opeeum." He winked. "Ver' bad."

At Islam-Qala, a clump of adobe buildings marked the actual frontier. As we got off the bus, a squad of customs men leapt on and began throwing off the cargo on the roof. Most of it consisted of huge bundles and crates belonging to the merchants, and the *douaniers* began ripping them open and rummaging through the contents, scattering cheap mirrors, sundry dry goods, and bolts of cloth in the dust, while the owners shouted in protest. The merchants were bold characters, tall and hawk-faced, Pathans from eastern Afghanistan. When they noticed the shabby, hobbit-sized Afghan Army sentry by the customs house grinning at their discomfiture, one of the Pathans pointed at the man and then stuck his finger in his fist and jerked it in and out; the Pathans whooped with glee, and at that the sentry burst into tears, and stood there in his suffocating four-sizes-too-big pre-Revolutionary Russian surplus woolen uniform, clutching his battered carbine, bawling like a baby. This was already a strange, strange land.

Inside the immigration office, an elastic man with squiggly eyes and a pencil-line mustache, who called himself "the Colonel," shouted "World War Three has begun!" The crowd of Westerners stared at him, aghast. "Yes, World War Three has begun," he yelled, and this time he laughed. "All the men must return to Iran, and the women must come with me!" He flung himself behind his desk and riffled through the stack of passports before him, collected on the way in by an underling. On the wall behind him, a poster drooped, held up by string and nails. VISIT SWITZERLAND it said, over a colorful scene of cows, a meadow, Alps.

The Colonel finished his perusal of our passports and fanned them on the desktop. Suddenly he assumed a sinister expression. "So-o-o-o," he hissed, like a villain in a bad movie. "Which of you are carrying hashish?" There were loud denials, protestations of innocence. "No hashish?" More denials. "Aha!" With a magician's flourish,

he reached into his desk drawer, produced a
kilo-size brick of hash, tossed it high in the air,
and caught it. A heavy smell of earthen sweetness
filled the room. He held the kilo out. "Who wants
to buy?" No one dared. A few minutes later, our
passports embellished, we were paying a bogus
doctor in the next room two dollars apiece not to
inject us with a horse syringe full of sticky green
syrup. If you didn't pay, and refused to be in-
jected, the "doctor" claimed you were violat-
ing some mythical World Health statute, and he
sent you back to Iran. It was a perfect scam.
The syringe looked like it hadn't been used in
years; it lay embedded in a hardened pool of
the green stuff, in a metal pan, covered with flies.
We paid, laughing; it was all so crazy, so funny, you couldn't help it. Welcome to Afghanistan!

There was more. From Islam-Qala, we caught
another minibus to the city of Herat. It was dusk
when we left, and soon we were driving through
darkness, by the light of two tenuous headlight
beams. Our fellow passengers had changed: the
merchants were gone, and we had picked up
another mob of tribesmen, even wilder looking
men, big turbans, big beards, rifles, and jangling
cartridge belts. I sat between a green-eyed Italian
girl with a ring in her nostril and a local Goliath
with an awesome orange-hennaed beard, who
stared at me from about eight inches away, smiling with benevolence and wonder. He beamed

and beamed at me as we hurtled eastward on the night road.

After a while, the bus driver, a little man in a ludicrous plaid polyester sports-car cap, cranked open the vehicle's windscreen, which swung on a horizontal pivot, to try to cool off the suffocating interior. A flying circus of moths and winged insects seethed in on the warm breeze; to protect his eyes, the driver snatched a pair of dark glasses off the face of a Frenchman sitting behind him, and jammed them on, ignoring the Frenchman's loud objections. The glasses kept the insects out of his eyes, but they also kept out the light. Blinded, the driver swerved off the narrow potholed tarmac into the desert. There were angry shouts from both Westerners and Afghans, but the driver gestured dismissively at us, barking an oath. I think he liked the way the foreign sunglasses went with his tatty Product of USSR cap.

One or two more seconds went by, as we caromed and tilted across the desert. Suddenly one of the tribesmen in the rear decided enough was enough. With an expletive he rose, bulled his way up the crowded aisle, raised his rifle, and brought the wooden butt down hard on the driver's skull. As the victim howled, the big man snatched the dark glasses from the man's face, crumpled them like paper in his enormous fist, and tossed them out the window. The driver struggled with the wheel and managed to muscle the vehicle back onto the pavement. The big tribesman harrumphed with satisfaction and headed back to his seat with the air of someone who has just Taken Care of Business. The Frenchman and the driver squawked angrily, and everyone else cheered, and we zoomed onward toward the ancient city of Herat.

Afghanistan in 1972 was a strange, paradoxical, complex little country. It scored close to the bottom on the UN's national per capita income scale, down in the neighborhood of Bangladesh, Upper Volta, and Chad. It was landlocked, arid, mostly mountainous. Its chief licit exports were dried fruits, pistachio nuts, and karakul sheepskins. Ninety percent of its seventeen million–odd people were subsistence farmers and herdsmen, members of tribal groups like the Ghilzais, Shjn-waris, Hazaras, Turkomans, and Aimaqs.

At the same time, there was little or none of the squalor or misery usually associated with the third world; in fact, Afghanistan had a kind of grandeur, richness. Deprived? You never would have associated the word with the Afghans. Two thirds of Afghanistan's peasants owned and tilled their own land, and big absentee landlords, the bane of most peasant societies, were few and far between. According to one estimate, fewer than thirty rural landowners possessed holdings of over five hundred acres. The average Afghan was a fiercely independent yeoman; he bowed only to Allah and *nang*, God and honor, and to no man at all.

This air of pride struck you with an almost palpable force. When British traveler and historian Robert Byron reached Afghanistan from Iran back in the 1930s, he wrote, "Here at last was Asia without an inferiority complex." He went on to describe the Afghan men he saw in the streets of Herat: "Hawk-eyed and eagle-beaked, the swarthy loose-knit men swing through the dark bazaar with a devil-may-care self-confidence." I saw the same men in Herat in 1972, felt the same assured and savage grace.

If anything, the impact was even more dramatic than in Byron's time, coming from an Iran that had reached a sort of terminal cultural distress, something between a massive inferiority complex, a total crisis of belief, and massive paradoxical xenophobia-cum-megalomania. The perfect image of Iran in 1972 was a youth in a pompadour and a cheap shiny suit, leering at a soft-core porno blonde on a poster in front of a theater in Teheran, his eyes blazing with lust and hatred and his lips muttering imprecations against the Decadent West. Afghans, you felt, would have either burned the theater to the ground or gone in and enjoyed the show. They knew what they were doing.

■   ■   ■

I hung out in Herat awhile, and the more time I spent there the more I liked the Afghans. Their seemingly boundless delight in themselves and their country produced some wonderfully perverse civic boasting. There were holy men everywhere in Afghanistan, my Herati friends told me, and their tombs were everywhere: the sarcophagus of one saint outside Herat was so holy that if you lay on the ground twenty paces away you would roll irresistibly toward it, pulled by the dead saint's magnetic power, till you fetched up against the walls of the sepulcher with a bump.

There are *tigers* in those mountains that *eat* people, someone else would say, as if he were boasting of a new hydroelectric project or his nation's first tractor factory. "In the Hindu Kush, the peaks are so high that even the eagles and vultures cannot fly over them. They must walk over the summits of the mountains, and the hunters wait there, hiding in rocks, and they shoot them!"

Time was another thing that struck you about Afghanistan: how old the place was, and how alive the past. I used to climb the brick minarets in the gardens of Queen Gawar Shad at sunset with my South African girlfriend and Hajji, the young manager of the Shark Hotel, where we were staying. We would look out over the city, the sea green minarets blazing, flocks of pigeons whirring up from a courtyard, a horse cart kicking up topaz puffs of dust . . . A scene out of Dreamtime, long ago. The gardens and spires were built in 1417, but Heratis spoke as if they knew the queen personally: "She was so beautiful, and she loved God so much, more than she loved any man . . ."

In the rambling old bazaar, you heard rumors of tribal warfare in the hills, of wolves attacking flocks ("Last winter, an old man was eaten alive, right on the outskirts of Herat!"). The caravans that formed up in the narrow lanes, bound west for Iran or east into the fastnesses of the Hazarajat or north onto the windy steppes of Turkestan, could have been five hundred, a thousand years old. What bound them to our fallen times?

They were hard people, these Afghans, hard as sand, but their hardness concealed a kernel of fey tenderness deep inside.

The nomads in the hills had had a terrible winter and spring, losing thousands of sheep, goats, and camels to deep snows, flash floods, mud. Destitute, they came to Herat, hordes of them, camping everywhere in their black low-slung tents. Disaster had not humbled them: even for Afghans they were wild-looking folk, the men with gaunt faces like scorched iron, the women bold-eyed as gypsies, blue tattoos on their cheeks, chin, brows, like star charts of unknown skies.

The nomads and the city people were traditionally less than friends—the former had a longstanding reputation for marauding, defrauding, and generally victimizing the latter—but the merchants and tradesman of Herat were feeding the nomads, giving them money. They had been doing it for weeks, and they would keep on doing it till the herdspeople had recovered enough to go on the trail again.

When I complimented them on their generosity, Heratis just shrugged: "It is our custom, we always help poor people. It is called *zakat* in the Holy Koran—those who have money and goods must share them with those who do not. We are only doing what we are supposed to do; that's all." But there was real warmth, kindness, behind the act of giving, you could see that.

I made so many friends, had so many delightful encounters in that old Afghanistan.

I remember going to look for a sheepskin hat in the bazaar in Herat, wandering into a narrow niche of a fur shop and being befriended by the two merchants and their corps of apprentices and shopboys. They invited me back again and again: long, drowsy days spent sipping green tea, *sheen chai*, out of tiny chipped porcelain cups, talking of Islam, Christianity, and Judaism, of men and women, capitalism and communism, tradition and progress, the meaning of life and the relationship of God to man. They never tired of pretending to trick me into converting to their faith. "Let me teach you our language," one of them would say, winking exaggeratedly at his companions. "Say after me—'*Allah illaha illala, Mohammeda rasulla*'—'There is one God, his name is Allah, and Mohammed is his prophet.' " When I repeated the words they would whoop triumphantly, and congratulate me for joining the True Faith. "You good Mussulman now!" and we would laugh and laugh together.

And who could forget the king of the camel merchants, a huge man with pockmarked cheeks and heavy epicanthic eyelids, who saw a photograph of my six-year-old daughter and asked if he could propose marriage to her "when she is old enough, by your custom—fifteen is old enough? I swear"—his big hand on his heart—"she will be the first and foremost of all my wives!" You couldn't help but like the man, he was so sincere, so heartfelt. From then on, whenever we met, he would place his hand on his breast and gaze at me mournfully, like Pavarotti about to launch into an aria of unrequited love. Alas, when I returned to America and told my daughter about it, she howled with glee.

Sometimes, the very extravagance of Afghanistan seemed to contain the mysterious marrow of meaning at the core of the country. In Kabul, a rotund little Turkoman from the far north in an enormous sky blue turban tried to sell me a footstool he claimed had belonged to Iskander, Alexander the Great; the king of kings, he said, had

21

used it to climb on and off his fabulous horse Bucephalus, and had somehow left it behind 2,297 years ago on his way across Afghanistan to conquer India. All of this seemed highly unlikely, since the stool was made of freshly varnished blond pine, nailed together with shiny galvanized nails. I couldn't help laughing: it was so perverse and outrageously unreasonable, as if someone tried to sell you King Arthur's Rolodex, or the Chris-Craft Caesar used to cross the Rubicon; but when I laughed, the Turkoman actually went into a rage, insisting on the stool's provenance in a voice that rose with rage to a batlike squeak: "EET BELONG TO EESKANDER! HE LEAVE EET—HE FORGET—"

The more he protested, the harder I laughed, of course, until finally he ordered me out of his shop. I stood in the dust of the street, still laughing, unable to stop—astounded, incredulous laughter: how could the Turkoman even begin to dare to pretend the stool was authentic—it was, in fact, the newest looking piece of furniture I had seen in all of Afghanistan—and then become so furious about it? I didn't understand, but it delighted me, and it seemed to fit in with everything else I was experiencing in Afghanistan. This was a land where spirits ran free and high and a fierce exuberance filled the very air, blowing away dry logic and dull reason, making almost anything seem possible.

▪   ▪   ▪

I loved Afghanistan, but it never stopped being strange; even now, after all the other times there in peace and war, it remains a puzzlement.

A lot of the feeling of mystery had to do with the virtual invisibility of half of the human race. Back in the 1970s, nomad and village women went unveiled in Afghanistan, but purdah was observed strictly in cities like Herat and Kandahar. When women appeared in public they went in the guise of ghosts, *afreets*, clad in the head-to-toe shrouds called burkahs, with a woven grillwork over the face.

Sometimes you brushed close to these apparitions in a narrow lane, on a bus, in the doorway to a shop, and you glimpsed a white ankle as slim as your wrist, a brocade slipper, and you inhaled the scent of flowers. Sometimes a whisper would just reach your ears, from behind the mask—*"Bonjour mister"*; "Hellowhat eesyourname?"—a whisper that seemed to contain all the longing of half a city, half a world.

I returned two more times, after that first visit in the summer of 1972: once the next winter, on my way back to Europe from the Himalayas, and again in 1975, on my way to a last hopeless stab at the Ph.D. thesis.

That last time, things were changing in Afghanistan. The king, Zahir Shah, had been overthrown by his cousin, Mohammed Daoud. The way people in Herat told it, the king and

Daoud had met at a cocktail party, argued, and Daoud had slapped his royal kinsman, whereupon the king burst into tears, drove straight to the airport, and flew off to Rome and abdication. The Ruritanian style of the tale was sublimely Afghan. Daoud had gone on to declare the country a republic, but no one I talked with in Herat seemed impressed by any of it: most Heratis were Persian-speaking Tajiks, and they regarded the activities of the Pushtu-speaking Pathans in the capital with something like bemused and bored contempt: "Those idiot Pathans are at it again." Eventually, Daoud's political machinations would lead to his own downfall and death, and, further down the road, the Soviet invasion, but no one could have dreamed any of that at the time. Afghanistan may have been changing, but the changes seemed insubstantial, phantom ripples on a depthless sea of still, golden sand.

Looking back now, knowing what I know, those final days in old Afghanistan take on a weight and color they never had originally, a mood of blue foreboding, bittersweet anguish. The king of the camel merchants still wanted to marry my daughter: "She is how old now? Ten years old? Good!" Riding the bus from Herat to Kandahar to Kabul was still a rude adventure, a magic-carpet ride slamming along on no shocks and cavernous potholes. The buses themselves set the tone for the entire journey: they were adorned with dangling chains, geegaws, ornaments, twinkling Christmas tree lights, and metal sculptures of jet planes and rockets, painted with rainbow murals of scimitars, Korans, bouquets, lions, mosques, and acrobatic calligraphy, till they looked like rolling collaborations by Edsel Ford, Red Grooms, and Nebuchadnezzar. No matter that they barely ran and were grossly uncomfortable, that wasn't the point; the Afghans demanded magnificence, *style*.

At two in the morning, crossing some cobblestone-and-gravel desert, some boneyard range, the driver would jam a tape in the dashboard cassette machine, savage music with hot, throbbing voices, crashing drums, thrashing strings (in Afghanistan, the love songs sounded like martial airs and the war songs like proclamations of universal destruction), and then twist the volume up all the way, way too loud, till the cheap speakers couldn't handle it anymore, and the sound melted down around the edges into pure deafening chaos. You rolled on through the night in a cloud of thunder while the driver turned and smiled at you, nodding and smiling as if to say, "Isn't this wonderful? Isn't this the most wonderful journey in the world?" Yes, it was.

Sometimes, in the night, you would smell a pang of greenness, wetness, on the wind, and a half hour or so later you would arrive at an oasis, a village, a caravanserai in the desert. There were flowers, trees, flowing water, crops leaning over the roadside ditches; as the bus pulled up in front of a teahouse, the street filled with people, kids hawking fruit and glasses of cloudy drinking water, men gawking in the windows at the foreigners on the bus, beating on the sides of the vehicle with tree limbs . . . All this sudden, vivid life in the middle of such empty desiccation had the quality of prestidigitation, a trick: all of Afghanistan, in fact, seemed something out of nothing, a glory of honor, faith, style, passion, conjured from a void of rock, dust, and thin air.

And now, of course, so much of it is gone forever . . .

two

n the years after Daoud's overthrow of Zahir Shah, Afghanistan drifted further and further into the Soviet orbit. Daoud allowed Marxist intellectuals and Moscow-trained military officers to move into key positions in the government, and he made the country more and more dependent on aid from the USSR, while downplaying relations with traditional Moslem allies like Turkey and Iran. As Soviet influence in Afghanistan grew, hundreds of Islamic religious leaders fled to Pakistan.

By 1978, even Daoud was having second thoughts about his nation's relationship with its giant neighbor to the north. He began a belated campaign to reestablish Afghanistan's sovereignty, but it was too late. In April 1978, Soviet-backed Marxists slaughtered Daoud, his family, and his supporters, and a "revolutionary regime" was set up, under longtime Afghan Marxist politicians Hafizullah Amin, Nur Mohammed Taraki, and Barbrak Karmal.

Over the next months the situation inside Afghanistan grew steadily worse. The leaders of the new government fought among themselves, while their repressive policies alienated more and more of the population. There were mass arrests and executions, and massacres of rebellious villagers. Tens of thousands of Afghans streamed across the borders into Iran and Pakistan. First Taraki and then Amin died violently at the hands of their own fellow revolutionaries. Uprisings spread across the countryside, from Herat in the west to the Khyber Pass in the east.

With their puppet regime in Kabul on the verge of collapse, the Soviets invoked their so-called Brezhnev doctrine, which stated that no country which had undergone a Marxist-Leninist revolution and entered the Soviet camp could be allowed to "regress" into independence. On Christmas Eve 1979, they launched a massive airborne and ground invasion, using their military power to install Barbrak Karmal as strongman in Kabul. As tanks and aircraft moved to crush resistance, the tide of refugees swelled. Within a year, more than four million Afghans would flee their homeland. Despite heavy losses the Afghan resistance fought on, aided by arms and supplies from the People's Republic of China, the United States, Pakistan, Saudi Arabia, and Egypt.

▪ ▪ ▪

The war had been going on for nearly five years
before I finally got the nerve to go back, in the
spring of 1984.

I had managed to miss Vietnam, partly by
accident, partly on purpose, mostly the latter. I
had clothed it all in the political rhetoric of the
time—"Stop the war!" "Peace now!"—but what
was really on my mind was a kaleidoscope of
images of bullets tearing into my frail flesh, fire
washing over me, explosions, agony, and annihilation. The simple truth was, I was terrified of
the idea of war. Now a country I knew and loved
was being destroyed, and still I held back, invent-
ing a million excuses.

Destiny chooses strange, unimaginable paths
for us. When I finally went, it was less a moral
decision, a conscious leap of courage, than a
weird confluence of chance events. My marriage
was disintegrating, and I despised my career as a
free-lance writer turning out escapist adventure-
travel yarns. There was a void in my life, one of
those empty spaces that pull you to jump.

In the midst of this, my cousin Robin returned from a stint as a combat photographer in
Lebanon. He was wired, whirring with Faustian
energy. He had shot the famous photographs of
the slaughter at Sabra and Shattila, and he joked
about it—"My pics are so good, you can just
about hear the flies buzz"—but you could tell it
had broken his heart and filled it with unhinged

passion. There was something almost grand about him, I thought.

We went surf-fishing together down on the Outer Banks of North Carolina. We stood on the night beach, drinking from a bottle of Bushmill's, casting out into the inky depths and hauling in flounder, spot, and sand sharks. I unhooked the sharks I caught and tossed them back, but when Robin pulled one in he beat it with a driftwood club till it stopped flapping and then buried it in the sand. They were small sharks, a foot or eighteen inches long, but he was taking no chances: "Don't throw them back, Rob. If you do, they'll grow up and come back and kill you someday."

I remember him telling me, with an air of great secrecy, that the world was being run by a cabal of evil old bearded men, Shiites and Orthodox Jews; they traveled around on intercontinental flying carpets, he said, hunting down people like Robin who trifled in their affairs. Somehow we got to talking about Afghanistan, and one of us, I'm not sure who, said, "Let's go."

From that point, things seemed to gain a momentum of their own. Robin and I pitched a story to *Time* magazine, where he was now a staff photographer; an in-depth piece on how one Afghan village had survived and suffered through the war. The editors liked it and said yes, though they didn't seem overcome with confidence in me: I had to pay my own way over and all my expenses, and when and if the story was finished *Time* would decide whether to buy it and for how much. Ah, the life of a stringer. No matter, I was ecstatic.

I cleaned out my meager savings account, packed up my sleeping bag, sneakers, and portable typewriter, bought a cheap, circuitous plane ticket, and headed off to war. I really had no idea what I was doing, what I was in for: part of me imagined my bloody corpse tumbled in a ditch somewhere in Afghanistan, another part imagined me returning with the Scoop of the Century, the Story That Drove the Russians out of Afghanistan. As I rode the jets from San Francisco to Bangkok, Bangkok to New Delhi, New Delhi to Lahore, these and other foolish thoughts fought endless battles in my mind.

Peshawar—the name means "City of Flowers"— was a dusty age-old garden bazaar at the base of the Khyber Pass, the gateway down from Central Asia to the riches of India. An endless procession of conquerors and empire builders, men like Alexander the Great, the Mogul Akbar, Babur the poet-king, the Greeks, the Persians, the Ghaznavids, Sikhs, and British, had fought their way through here and made the city theirs for a time, but always Peshawar remained, in its soul of secret souls, the city of the Pathans, the great tribal people who ruled the Khyber and spilled

across the borders of Afghanistan and Pakistan's North-West Frontier Province. Dynasties
bloomed and withered, rose and then toppled into
dust, but Peshawar and the Pathans endured.

Back in the 1970s, when I had passed
through Peshawar on my journeys, the place had
been at peace. Buses and trucks, camel caravans
and horse trains, crossed over the Khyber from
Afghanistan; travelers and traders passed through
on their way to Rawalpindi, Lahore, the borders
of India, and beyond. The gaudy young Westerners on their way to Kathmandu, nirvana, the ultimate fix, hardly raised a ripple. Peshawar had
seen it all before.

Now the war had come to Peshawar. Hundreds of thousands of displaced Afghans thronged
the city, crammed in crowded flats in Fakirabad
and the Old Bazaar, in refugee camps on the
outskirts of town, or camped in ragged tents and
makeshift lean-tos in vacant lots and rubbish
dumps. They were a cross section of the entire
Afghan nation: Westernized Kabuli intellectuals
in shiny big-shouldered suits, Mongol-looking
Turkomans from the north with horses to ride and
carpets to sell, tough little slit-eyed Shiite Nazar-
as, gaunt-faced nomad women from the caravan routes of Zabul and Ghazni, tall, spindly
Nuristanis from "the Valley of Light," blustery
Kandaharis, Pathans with pale fiery eyes . . .
Afghanistan was hemorrhaging, bleeding to
death, and this was its living blood, flowing

from sundered villages and terrorized cities and towns.

Along with the refugees had come the resistance: virtually all the mujahedin groups, and there were many, were headquartered in Peshawar, everything from NIFA, the National Islamic Front of Afghanistan, headed by a suave Sufi holy man who had been Kabul's Peugeot dealer before the war, to the populist Tajik-dominated Jamiat-i-Islami, to truly eccentric splinter groups such as anticommunist Nuristani separatists, the remnants of prewar Maoist student parties, Shiites who liked the Ayatollah Khomeini and Shiites who loathed him, and so on. Even by Afghan standards, the guerrilla leaders in Pakistan were an odd lot. Most of them owed whatever power they had to being in the right place at the right time: showing up in Pakistan in '79 and '80, when the flow of foreign assistance to the muj began, and donor nations were looking for someone, anyone, to channel the aid through. At their worst, they were really, really bad: atavistic tribal bosses, turn-the-clock-back-to-feudalism mullahs, deranged pro-Libyan crackpots. To find the pure soul of the resistance you had to look lower, further, at the corps of idealistic young guerrilla political and press officers, at the daredevil commanders and faithful masses inside Afghanistan who actually fought the war.

There was a colorful foreign expatriate community in Peshawar as well, drawn there by the war: the aid groups—UNHCR, UNDP, IRC, AID, IMC, ICRC, the Red Crescent, *Médecins sans frontières*, *Médecine du monde* and *Aide médicale internationale*, British Afghanaid, the Swedish Committee, and the German Committee; quixotes, Moonies, idealists, and profiteers. Along with the would-be mercenaries with their gaudy patter ("We went twenty clicks, then we ran into Ivan and stepped in some shit"), the spooks and spies, some real, mostly not, and the journalists, it was quite a scene. The last were mostly fringe characters like me, stringers, free-lancers, drifters with battered cameras and melted-down credit cards; the respectable main-stream press rarely made it as far as Peshawar. Waugh would have relished it all.

It was an edgy scene, with teeth. You didn't have to look far to find something to disturb you, make you afraid. The wounded were everywhere. They walked the dusty streets on crutches, swing-ing leg stumps, waving handless arms; they rolled along in rickety wheelchairs. In the hospitals, you could find room after room crowded with muti-lated men and boys; there were as many or more wounded women and girls, of course—mines and bombs didn't care—but you weren't allowed in their hospitals, and perhaps it was just as well. See one big-eyed kid with a leg missing below the knee, a lopped-off arm, a slender back turned to raw craterous scar tissue by napalm or phospho-rus and you've seen enough, way, way too much.

There was violence, the real thing, in Peshawar, too. Bombs went off almost every day, planted by agents of Khad, the Afghan surrogate of the KGB; resistance commanders and leaders were assassinated, blown away by Kalashnikov fire at bus stops, on the sidewalk in broad daylight. An outlaw Khyber Pass Pathan tribe called the Kukikhels added to it all with their own bombing campaign. Angered when the Pakistani Army bulldozed a number of their heroin labs up on the Khyber, the Kukikhels blew up several local landmarks, topping off with a gigantic dynamite bomb that leveled the Peshawar railway station. No one was killed, reportedly because the Kukikhels left the bomb (it was huge, a crate of TNT) in plain view in the middle of the terminal, with a two-hour timer and a sign that read something like: THIS IS A BOMB. SIGNED, THE KUKIKHELS. They didn't want to kill any members of rival tribes—Adamkhels, Suleimankhels, or whatever—after all; that would ignite a *badal*, a blood feud, with the members of the slain man's tribe, and the Kukikhels only wanted to send a message to the government of Pakistan.

When you threw in the war stories that were everywhere, on everyone's lips, in mujahedin newsletters and the local Pak papers, there was no escape. Every day you heard a dozen more, whether you really wanted to or not: a massacre by Soviet commandos in Badakshan; a nomad caravan decimated by gunships; a mosque torched

in Paktia; a muj ambush in Kandahar, a tank
knocked out and a famous commander martyred
in the firefight that followed. *Martyred,* not killed:
you soon learned that this was a Holy War, and in
a Holy War the dead did not merely die. In the
spring of 1984, most of the news from the war was
bad, but you got it anyway. The war came at you
in a hail of invisible shrapnel that ripped through
you without leaving a trace. No one could see, but
you knew, you knew.

You knew fear, and sorrow, but you also began to
taste the twisted beauty that wars kindle, in the
form of spectacular people, extreme people, people you loved on sight or goggled at with sheer
incredulity, the blessed and the perishing bright-
est, lit with the loveliest of lost and perilous
causes.

There was the pretty, wistful young Dutch
woman, who wore a heart-shaped locket defiantly
inscribed BREAK IT. She raised money in Europe,
flew to Pakistan, walked deep into Afghanistan
and gave the cash away to widows, orphans,
wounded civilians. There was Lech, the gaunt
Polish expatriate, who tried to instruct the mujahedin in unarmed combat. "Come at me with a
knife," he told a young guerrilla; the guerrilla
did, wriggled through Lech's attempted jujitsu
moves, and, to his own embarrassment and
shame, managed to stick the blade through Lech's

forearm. The Pole wore a huge lumpy bandage for
months. Later he would die mysteriously in the
wilds of Nuristan, killed either by renegade mujahedin or in a fall off a mountain. And how could
I ever forget the flamboyant little commander from
Zabul, who wore a gigantic oversize turban, sultry
eye shadow, and Chanel No. 5, and careened
around Peshawar in a captured Russian jeep with
a bullet hole through the windshield and a
daredevil teenage mujahed behind the wheel?
One day they careened too far, ran over a group of
Pakistani pedestrians, and were booted back
across the border into the war with orders never to
return.

By far the most dramatic of my new Afghan
friends was Mohammed Azeem, a huge, shambling, shaggy Pan-like mujahed who had been a
hippie in Kabul before the war; he owed his
gigantic beard and flowing locks to a vow he had
made, not to cut either till communism was driven
out of Afghanistan. He was a virtuoso flutist, and
he could play for hours, from dusk till dawn,
spinning out endless wild melodies, pausing only
to puff hashish smoke for inspiration. Despite his
Rasputin- or yeti-like appearance, the man had a
heart as pure as a babe's. Shortly after I met him,
I gave him an extra pair of hiking boots. They
barely squeezed over his enormous splayed feet,
but he was so moved that he seized me in his long
arms and began to weep; hot tears rained down on
the top of my head. The next day, as I made my

rounds through Peshawar, every Afghan I met heaped praise on me for my generosity toward Azeem. It was mortifying. He must have run through the city all night long, shouting news of my gift.

Among all my new friends, one stood out with a special grandeur: Professor Burhauddin Majrooh. Tall, disheveled, yet with a strange ethereal elegance, limping on a game leg, his hair a white Einsteinian halo, this gentle, good man was the spiritual paterfamilias of the Jihad in Peshawar. Through his Afghan Information Center, headquartered in a succession of down-at-the-heels villas out in the University Town section of the city, Majrooh tried to explain the Afghan resistance and its war to the outside world, using everything from Kant and Hegel to Afghan folk stories and fairy tales. He painstakingly collected battlefield reports from refugees, mujahedin, and foreign reporters and aid workers, and published them in monthly photocopied pamphlets. He was the war's weary master scribe, the world's scorned conscience. I would never forget the hours I spent with Majrooh, drinking tea, talking about the Holy War, its tragedies and triumphs, its chances of survival. Despite his erudition and sophistication, Majrooh never lost his intense sympathy for the illiterate, ardently religious rural masses who were actually doing most of the fighting.

▪   ▪   ▪

Life at the edge of the war went on. I stayed at
Dean's Hotel, on Saddar Road, on the vague
borderline between the new and old cities. Its
walled compound of rambling gardens and dingy
cavernous suites had a certain charm, attenuated
by the truly appalling food: mummified chicken
cutlets, warm soda, tinned mystery vegetables,
rock-hard rolls, wine-dark tea like battery acid.
Dean's was also notorious for its sinister scrutiny
of the journalists and other foreigners who stayed
there. Half the hotel staff were reputedly Pakistani ISI agents, and both the phones and the
rooms themselves were bugged. There was a story
about two American journalists who were confer-
ring in their room when the heavy framed picture
of Mount Fujiyama above them on the wall suddenly emitted an ear-splitting blast of feedback,
scaring them half out of their wits.

Riding with the notorious hotel driver, "Gooj-
er," a rotund, unkempt rascal who reported my
every move to the Pakistani authorities and grossly overcharged me, I continued my pursuit of the
story. Mostly on my own: Robin rotated back and
forth from the Philippines, where he was working
on another *Time* assignment. I spent day after
day, week after week, prowling the refugee camps
around Peshawar, trying to find the archetypal
village for the article. Finally, I settled on a place
called Dobanday, in the western foothills of the
Safed Koh Mountains, the White Mountains, a
two- or three-day journey from the border. It had

been one of the first Afghan villages to be heavily involved in the war, way back in 1978, even before the Soviet invasion. Because of its key position on the border trade and infiltration routes, Dobanday was attacked relentlessly with aircraft and armor. Finally, one cold winter night, the people decided to go to Pakistan.

One of the elders told me the story: "There was a ring around the moon," he said. "The air was full of ice. All the dogs in the town were howling; they knew something bad was happening. We loaded our families on our horses and trucks, and started over the mountains to Pakistan." Helicopters and jets continued to bombard the villagers over the next two days, as they traveled toward the border. As they crossed the last pass, down toward the border town of Terri Mangal, a blizzard struck. The Dobanday folk trudged the last few miles in swirling snow. "When we reached Terri Mangal," the old man said, "someone said that we had left Afghanistan, our homeland, behind. Two young girls heard this, and they fell over and died there in the snow. The sorrow of leaving their homes killed them."

Now, six years later, almost all of Dobanday's four or five thousand people were still living in the camps near Peshawar, part of the horde of four million Afghan refugees in Pakistan and Iran. Some of the men went back periodically to fight, camping out in the ruins and raiding down onto the plains of Logar to the west. The people of Dobanday were not the fiercest of Afghans, but their story—of loss, displacement, exile, clinging to faith—seemed to me to be one of the essential stories of the war.

And then, before I knew it, it was time to go and see.

three

oing to the war turned out to be like nothing I could have possibly dreamed or imagined. Of course: what did I expect?

Robin and I left around midnight, dressed in our baggy Afghan clothes, traveling with a translator-guide named Mister Etibari, "the trustworthy one." We rode in a mujahedin jeep to the house of Brigadier Safi, the guerrilla leader who was supposed to take us to the border; it was an endless drive, burrowing down ever narrower lanes and alleys, but when we got there the brigadier was gone. We waited fruitlessly in a dusty moonlit garden full of strutting insomniac peacocks, watched by a guard with an antique carbine. Finally, Mister Etibari gave up: "Let's try Brigadier Safi's camp," he sighed. "Maybe he is there."

Soon we were speeding south out of the city, into the off-limits zone of the Tribal Area. We passed through a Pakistani Army roadblock, then turned off onto an unpaved track. A few minutes later, we arrived at a compound guarded by Afghan sentries. Rows of canvas tents extended into the distance. In the open area between, something like a riot was going on. Several hundred men were milling around, shouting, waving fists, banners, sticks, while a political officer stood on a truck and harangued them through a bullhorn. A moment later we were in Brigadier Safi's tent, drinking tea with the man; he had a clipped mustache and a highly polished bald cranium, and he boasted that he was the only man in the world who had been trained by the Special Forces of the United States, Great Britain, and the USSR, all three. A few minutes later we were bundled onto a decrepit bus with about a hundred of the riotous Afghans. There were six buses in all, and each, like ours, was loaded to double its capacity. The troop convoy—for that was what it was: these guerrillas, just trained, were going home to fight—groaned out onto the road, the long road to the frontier.

The terrible road to the frontier, that night: I kept thinking that if the war were half as bad as the journey to it, then we were doomed. Robin and I were jammed in between the muj so tightly our ribs creaked and it was hard to breathe, and the trip seemed to go on forever in the sluggish, slumping vehicles. We couldn't stop: if the Pakistani soldiers and police manning the myriad checkpoints caught Robin and me, we would be

sent back to Peshawar and tossed in jail. Inexplicable Third World politics: the Pakistanis
backed the Afghan resistance and wanted their
struggle publicized, but did their best to nail
journalists covering the war. No one ever figured
it out. Worse, tribesmen paid by the Soviets and
the Kabul government had been ambushing
Afghan resistance convoys in the Tribal Area,
where the Pakistani government held a measure of
power only through force of arms and suasion, and
feuding Pathan tribes did what they willed. It was
a crazy danger zone. On and on we went, through
the outlaw town of Darra Adam Khel, with its
dope shops and arms bazaar selling assassins' pen
guns and pistols, AK-47s and rockets, brown
heroin and pungent green marijuana; up over the
switchbacks and cruel, stony heights of Kohat
Pass; through Kohat, Thal, and paranoid, terrify-
ing Paracheenar . . .

Sometime just after dawn the buses halted;
I vaguely remember everyone staggering off
through a field to a ditch to drink and wash, and
the Afghans praying toward Mecca, and then we
were traveling again, up a rocky and desolate
valley toward the frontier. Spiky snow-dusted
mountains loomed to the north and west now:
Afghanistan. The pink of dawning bloomed into
blue skies, the sun blazed down on us, and then
we were lurching into the border town of Terri
Mangal, named, Mister Etibari informed us, after
two local tribes, the Terris and the Mangals, who

loathed each other and feuded and fought incessantly. The Afghan frontier lay just above, on
the crest of the ridge to the west.

There was just time to register a scatter of
images, a rutted street, scowling armed men, a
stall selling Chinese hand grenades and what
looked like pancakes and bread loaves of gray
putty and were surely hashish, ranks of chocka-
block teahouses, shops, and God knows what, the
offices of the Independent Bandits for World
Islam and the Hashasheen Holding Company,
and then we were off the bus and being propelled
up a ladder, into an upstairs room.

There were carpets, cushions, and, miracu-
lously, there was Brigadier Safi again. He shook
our hands warmly: "Welcome!" Before Robin and
I had a chance to congratulate each other on
making it this far, a mujahed burst in the door.
"*Pakistani police!*" he hissed. Before we could
react, two burly guerrillas pushed us to the floor,
grabbed up an overstuffed mattress, tossed it on
top of us, and sat down on the whole assemblage,
just as a pair of gimlet-eyed uniformed Pakistanis
entered the room.

We lay there, crushed, smothered. The hero-
ic war correspondents. Eternities went by. Every
so often an obscenity escaped Robin's lips, and
who could blame him? I heard the muffled clink
of teacups, idle pleasantries, yawns, as Brigadier
Safi and his aides entertained the police. It really
was beyond belief. Didn't the Pakistanis notice

something odd about the mattress? Couldn't Safi just baksheesh them, bribe them, pay them to go away? But that would have made too much sense: we were part of some absurd deceit, the men who weren't really there, now you see them now you don't, and there was no escape.

At last, we heard the Pakistanis leave: "Go safely." "Go with God." "May Allah favor your path." I felt the two sitters rise, and then the mattress was lifted, and we looked up into a circle of guileless, expectantly smiling faces.

"You like green tea, black tea?"

four

We cross that afternoon.

The border is invisible, of course, an imaginary line on the ridge by a fortified Pakistani Army outpost, but we know when we pass through: Mister Etibari and the mujahedin from Dobanday hold their open palms toward the heavens, lips moving in silent prayer, thanking Allah for allowing them home again. Past stands of pine, down a narrow granite defile by a rushing stream, and then we see the first signs of war: a fire-gutted concrete building shot full of holes (it was a sawmill before the war, the mujahedin say), the burned-out shell of a Soviet armored personnel carrier. This is it, I tell myself: this is what you have been waiting for, what you have heard so much about. You are Inside now.

It begins to drizzle as we emerge onto a high plateau ringed by mountains to the north, south, and east. There are adobe ruins scattered in the distance, a zigzag abandoned trenchline, more corpses of slain armor. There has been much

fighting here, many, many battles, Mister Etibari
tells me. The big Soviet/Afghan Army fire base of
Jaji is just over the moors to the west, and enemy
convoys sweep across the mountains every few
months, fighting to try to cut the resistance supply
lines from Pakistan. This is bloody ground, rinsed
in fire. Hundreds have died here.

As we travel on into the evening, we pass one
bombed-out, devastated village after another:
empty courtyards, shattered rooms, dead gardens,
fallow fields. In one place, a cluster of high
explosive bombs have sundered an irrigation ca-
nal, and the waters boil across the trail and flood
the fields beyond. In another place, an entire
orchard, peach trees and apple trees, has been
smashed by cluster bombs and rockets. In another
lost village, the mujahedin show me the black-
ened shell of the schoolhouse. Soviet airborne
troops landed here, and were driven away by the
local guerrillas. As they retreated, the Soviets
torched the school. The floor is still littered with
lessons and copybooks, left behind by the fleeing
children. Among them, I find childish scrawled
alphabets, crayon drawings of bouquets and kit-
tens. Everyone is gone now, of course, in exile in
Pakistan, or dead.

I will never get used to these desecrated
places: there is something about them, a sense of
tremendous sorrow, evil, and excruciating injustice, that will stick in my throat forever. You

can see the ingenuity, the instinct for beauty and backbreaking labor that went into building them: terraced fields scratched out of stone-pudding soil, sweet orchards grown from snowmelt captured in webs of hard-won ditches, houses with adobe walls three feet thick, with roofbeams as big around as a man hauled from twenty miles away, with doors and windows carved into lace-like filigree. They planted saplings in their courtyards, and flowerbeds by the gate; now the trees are dead of thirst, the flowers parchment, turning to dust. "Don't walk in the fields," Mister Etibari says. "There are butterfly mines everywhere. The Shurovee drop them from airplanes and helicopters, by the thousands." Everything is ruined.

As night falls, we take shelter in a village hidden away in the mouth of a canyon. Perhaps because of its location, or pure luck, it has escaped bombing and bombardment, unscathed. Many mujahedin are sheltering here overnight; in this blighted landscape, comfort and mercy are rare things.

After dinner, we join the villagers on the rooftops for the nightly entertainment. The whole village is there, right down to the children, newborn infants in their mothers' arms. We face west, down-valley, gazing off into the darkness. Suddenly, a scarlet spark arcs across the night, followed by another, and another. There are murmurs and exclamations of appreciation from the crowd as more loops of fire crisscross out there in the distance, punctuated by flashes of white light, all in perfect silence.

"Jaji," Mister Etibari explains. "The mujahedin are attacking Jaji. The red fire are Dashakas"—Chinese- and Soviet-made DshK 12.7-mm machine guns, firing tracers—"and the white fire, those are mortar shells."

"Mujahedin?"

"No. The mujahedin have no heavy mortars."

We watch as the firefight goes on, the machine guns firing and counterfiring tracers, the muj on the mountains, the Soviets and Kabul regime troops in their fortified bunkers on the valley floor, the kaffir mortars shelling the faithful. The faces of the villagers are rapt, enthralled. How many hundreds of nights have they watched this serpentine light show, the ancient neverending battle against the invaders, the violence that could reach out and destroy them in an instant? What can they be thinking?

For the next few days, we travel north and then west across the Safed Koh. The mujahedin from Dobanday have chosen this circuitous route to avoid the fortress at Jaji and its far-reaching harassment-and-interdiction fire. Still, there is no escaping the presence of the enemy. The skies above us buzz perpetually with his lethal presence: Antonov prop-driven spotter planes (reputed to carry infrared night-imaging gear and cameras that can capture a recognizable portrait of you from five miles up); MI-24 helicopter gunships, with their 170 air-to-surface rockets, two half-ton bombs, cannons firing six hundred rounds per minute; old MIGs, new MIGs, slick state-of-the-art Sukhois, packing a thousand kinds of supersonic annihilation. There is plenty to go around: a single two-chopper team of MI-24s can blow away an entire two-thousand-year-old village in less than three minutes. Even in these winding mazes of wadi and gorge, these remote fastnesses of mountain, the enemy and his dreams of slaughter are never far away . . . Just a shot away, always.

The odds against them are impossible; still, they are everywhere and undaunted, these mujahedin, holy warriors. Ninety-year-old great-grandfathers lugging one-hundred-and-thirty-year-old muzzle-loaders that originally knocked over the British troopers of Queen Victoria; smooth-cheeked twelve-year-olds armed with Egyptian AK-47s bought on the black market in Darra Adam Khel with the family savings. Farmers, truck drivers, schoolteachers, shepherds, mullahs—they come from sacked villages and ravaged farmsteads, but you almost always find them smiling.

These muj are powerfully simple folk. Ask them why they are fighting and they reply, *"Alla-ho akbar!"*—"God is great!" By this they mean,

"Only God is great; the things of man are ul-
timately poor, fleeting, decaying things, except in
that they partake of the righteousness of God, and
anyone who does not know this is a soulless
brute." As avowedly militant atheists, the Soviets
are like monsters out of an ultimate Afghan nightmare. Azeem back in Peshawar summed it up this
way, when I asked him about the Sovs: "They
fuck their mothers, they fuck their sisters." It was
partly pejorative, of course, but like everything
the Afghans say it spins off into a whole tapestry
of truths and semitruths: without Allah, without
belief in the human spirit, what limits are there on
the degradation of humanity? Once you go down
that twentieth-century path of man as industrial
meat puppet the depths know no bounds, there's
no stopping, nothing to hold on to . . . So the
Afghans believe. As men whose own natural wildness is constantly reined in by faith and ritual,
they know all about the possibilities of good and
evil.

They hold these beliefs with absolute, life-
and-death passion, enough to die for them a
thousand times. "Every Shurovee killed in Afghanistan is plunged straight into the fires of
eternal Hell," a mujahed tells me; "And every
one of the Faithful martyred goes straight to paradise." And he goes on to quote from the Koran:
" 'If there are ten of you against one hundred of
the faithless, you will prevail; and if there are a
hundred of you against ten thousand of the faith-

less, have no fear, for victory will be yours.' " He
nods and smiles at me: see the wondrous ways of
Allah? But I wonder, still, how long they can
survive.

Around midday, we reach the edge of the Safed
Koh highlands. The foothills and plateaus to the
west descend to the green plains of Logar; to the
north, beyond more jumbled summits, we can
make out the smudgy gray sprawl of Kabul, the
capital of Soviet Afghanistan. Directly below us,
the trail drops almost straight down into the gorge
that conceals Dobanday. We start down, sliding
and stumbling on the steep gravel and dirt slopes.
It feels safer, the deeper we descend, but that is
an illusion. At the bottom is the easternmost
house of Dobanday, a large, high-walled, flat-
roofed compound; it has been hammered, battered, whacked by rockets, bomb fragments, and
aerial artillery into wreckage, an instant archeo-
logical site.

Dobanday is built along miles of winding
canyon floor: rows of cliffhouses, blocks of
teashops, a towered mosque here and there . . .
Every single building has been damaged or destroyed. "Here," a mujahed tells us, "the Shurovee and the government soldiers came and
burned the mosque. I saw it with my own eyes!
The Shurovee officer came outside carrying the
Holy Koran. He tore it in pieces and threw the
pieces on the ground and stamped on them with

his boots. He was laughing!" It is the kind of story that may not have happened exactly the way it is told, but everyone believes it, knows the essential truth within, and the outrage it invokes transforms defeat into a kind of weapon. "They burned the mosque! They defiled the Holy Koran!" These are crimes that will not be forgiven for centuries, perhaps never.

Dobanday may have been destroyed, but it has not surrendered. Hundreds of mujahedin from the north and west shelter here, on their way home with weapons newly purchased in Pakistan. As night falls, they leave the comparative safety of the canyon and continue on across the perilous plains of Logar. One group we meet numbers close to nine hundred; they are from Badakshan, way up by the border of the Soviet Union, a seventeen-day journey from Dobanday. You wonder how many of them will make it home alive.

One thing you never forget: this is a Holy War. If you don't believe it, the Afghans will prove it to you.

On a hot, cloudless afternoon, the mujahedin lead us to a stone sarcophagus, in the midst of more bombed buildings. "If you are pure in your heart and you are killed in Jihad," they tell us, "your body will not decay." They pry loose a slab in one of the walls, and one man tilts a mirror to reflect the sun's light inside. "He was killed two years ago," someone says, as first Robin and then I peer through the hole. There, in the dim golden glow swimming with motes of illuminated dust, lies the body of a young man. Not mummified, not dried up and stiff: something else. He looks so perfect, so warm and animate, that you expect him to turn his head and smile at you, to yawn, stretch his arms and legs, and rise.

So far we have not found the enemy and he has not found us. We have had to hide from helicopter gunships and Antonovs a few times, and jets and choppers have overflown us at high altitude almost constantly, but no one has fired a shot our way. That is fine with me, actually: I tell myself I have been Inside, and that is enough. But Robin argues otherwise. You haven't really been to war, he insists, until you've been under fire, and our journey will be incomplete, bogus, unless we taste at least a hint of authentic action. He *knows,* I guess. Long before Beirut he shot combat pics in Vietnam, and his favorite Nam story is of a B-52 strike on the Cambodian border, and a group of crazed Khmer mercenaries tramping out of the blasted jungle eating the livers cut from dead North Vietnamese soldiers . . . The heart of darkness of war, and he has seen it, a wisdom that is a kind of damage; I have not. He wants us to take a different route back to Pakistan, close to the enemy base at Jaji, through the fighting there. I disagree violently, my fears taking over, but Robin manages to persuade Mister Etibari and the other Afghans to take the Jaji route. I am furious, the fury of panic, but I have no choice. What can I do? Of course, looking back on it, Robin is right: if you are going to go to war, then for God's sake do it.

We leave Dobanday, cross the desert highlands, and turn down the canyon that leads toward Jaji. By the second evening we reach a village, actually a small town, a few miles from the enemy base. The place is completely unscarred; obviously, the people here have reached some sort of accord with the occupiers and invaders. A pall of paranoia and betrayal hangs in the air. Evil eyes follow us as we walk through the streets; our mujahedin escorts finger their triggers, mutter under their breath. We spend an uneasy afternoon and evening in a resistance safe house at the edge of town, with sentries outside watching for trouble. Just after nightfall, we hear gunfire and explosions from the east: the nightly muj attack on the enemy fortress, the nightly enemy shelling of guerrillas and refugees on the mountain trails around Jaji. Toward midnight, it dies down. It is time to go.

We walk out into the most glorious night I have ever known. The sky blazes with stars, and the incense of pine forests smolders on the cold mountain wind. We trudge up the trail out of the village, walking carefully, communicating by signs and the softest of whispers. There are Soviet and Afghan Army patrols on these trails some-

times, the muj have warned us, and militia
ambush squads. We must be careful. Robin and I
may well have been spotted by enemy agents back
in the town, and there is a bounty for foreigners,
journalists, doctors, aid workers, traveling with
the resistance. Strangely, all of this only adds to
the feeling of calm mystery, mysterious calm, that
has come over me: as if we have all been here
before, and everything turned out well then and
will again. Am I demented, stressed out, or flash-
ing on wild truths?

We cross tumbling streams, climb through
steep timber, and then we come out into an open,
bowl-shaped valley. There it is: Jaji, incredibly
close, less than a quarter of a mile away. We see
arc lights burning, concertina wire, the blunt
outlines of bunkers and blockhouses. Guard dogs
catch our scent and begin to bay. I can just make
out the faint subterranean drone of generators.

We move on, almost tiptoeing, keeping to the
very center of the trail; there are mines all around
us, the muj say. It seems almost impossible that
we haven't been detected, the enemy is so near.
Surely the Soviets have Starlight scopes, infrared,
sound-monitoring devices, chemical sniffers? But
somehow, nothing happens.

We are climbing the mountainside beyond
the fortress. Robin, Mister Etibari and most of the
mujahedin are up ahead; another one or two muj
bring up the rear, somewhere behind me. I walk
alone, a stretch of trail that looks like a tunnel

through the starlit trees and rocks. And then
everything blows. Suddenly, a heavy machine gun
opens fire. I dive on my face in the pine needles
and humus, and lie there as more bursts of fire rip
the night. What the hell do I do now? The question is answered when one of the guerrillas from
the rear appears next to me and pulls me to my
feet; then we are running together, crouched low
to the ground. We race straight toward the machine gun and past it, *under* it, the bullets zinging
above our heads—militia? traitorous muj? madmen in the night? we never find out—just as a
heavy mortar begins lobbing illumination rounds
onto the mountainside below. We run and run, till
my lungs threaten to burst and I taste blood.

I hear the mujahed laughing now, like an
errant schoolboy caught out in some prankish
adventure, and I start laughing too, as we race
over the roof of the mountain and tumble down the
other side. The sounds of battle fade away behind. I can hear Mister Etibari, Robin, and the
others calling to us from below. A scrap of poetry,
Kipling, flies through my mind: "The night we
stormed Valhalla, ten thousand years ago . . ."
What could be sweeter, more epic, than traveling
with these good men, twining my destiny with
theirs, having evil men try to kill us, having them
fail? And now I will bring the story of this terrible
war to the world. I have never been so happy in
my life.

five

filed my story at the *Time* bureau in Bangkok, flew back to the States, and promptly
plummeted into a chasm of weirdness and
depression.

Before I went into the Afghan War, I had
thought it would be a kind of solution: that if I
forced myself to go in and then survived, I would
be rewarded with a measure of happiness and
inner peace. It was the worst kind of American
false mythologizing, of course, too much John
Wayne on the brain; and now, it turned out, I got
the opposite of what I expected.

The weirdness took many forms. For one
thing, I couldn't sleep; I sat up night after night,
my heart pounding, eyes bulging, waiting for the
throb of helicopter gunships, the rumble of shells.
I flicked across the cable stations with the remote
tuner incessantly, one A.M., two A.M., sickening
three and dread four, when you knew another
night's sleep was shot, bad dreams of the war
mingling with insane, inane American media im-

ages, a wriggling Madonna and a bloodthirsty
gunship, golfers strolling the greens at Palm
Springs and a caravan crawling away over hopeless hills, beneath lethal skies . . . juxtapositions
that made my skull feel like it was going to split in
half.

There were all kinds of feelings I couldn't
turn off, though I desperately wanted to. Driving
across country, I found myself dreaming ambushes everywhere: planning where to set the
mines, where to place the RPG to knock out key
vehicles quickly, the 12.7- and 14.5-mm machine guns for overlapping fields of fire and no
dead ground, and routes to scatter and escape the
helicopter strikes that were sure to follow. It was
foolish and deranged and vaguely vicious, visions
of tactical slaughter in the bucolic suburbs and
farmlands of peacetime America, but I couldn't
help it, my mind just wouldn't stop, it kept running on.

Beneath it all was a rage that burned out of
control: at the injustice of the war itself, at the
fact that no one in America seemed to want to
hear about it, and beyond that a general, free-
form, omnidirectional rage, tangled with gloom. I
felt as if a great secret had been entrusted to me in
Afghanistan, but that I had no one to tell it to. I
felt estranged, alienated; my old life in America
didn't make sense anymore, I couldn't connect
with it. To my surprise, I found myself thinking of
going back, wanting to go back to the war. I began

to feel as if I belonged there, where there were things worth dying for, worth living for, great men, grand causes. America in the Reagan era seemed small and shabby and devoid of magic.

I lined up a few assignments, I scraped together a little money, and by early winter I was on my way back over. I spent only three or four days in Peshawar this time, and then I was off, along with Mister Etibari again, on the long trek across the Tribal Area, north over the Safed Koh Mountains toward a place called Jegdeleg.

Professor Majrooh had warned me back in Peshawar how badly the war was going, but it was still shocking and depressing. The Soviets seemed to have turned the power and pressure up several notches since Robin and I had traveled Inside a few months earlier. There seemed to be three or four times as many enemy aircraft as before; they were everywhere, swarms of them. All the news we heard along the trail was bad, bad: the enemy was on the attack everywhere, tanks and infantry moving into the northern Safed Koh, airborne commandos landing in the mountain sanctuaries around us, and bombing, bombing, bombing. Just five days earlier, Soviet troops had fought their way into Jegdeleg itself and had held the town for the better part of a day before pulling out. The trail was jammed with refugees, thousands of them, heading for Pakistan.

What hadn't changed, hadn't gone down, was the Afghans' attitude. Most of the refugees we met on the trail were from around Soroobi, northwest of Jegdeleg, and theirs was an interesting story. The Afghan government had paid the tribes in the Soroobi area to help guard the hydroelectric lines leading to Kabul. They did so the first five years of the war, and then the tribal elders and chiefs decided enough was enough. They went to the mujahedin, borrowed a load of explosives, and proceeded to blow up more than two hundred power-line pylons in a single night, totally blacking out the Afghan capital. Now the Soviets were wreaking their vengeance, methodically bombing the turncoat villages flat, and the people were fleeing to Pakistan.

Still, in true Afghan style, the villagers had managed to salvage something essential from the catastrophe. They had made off with leagues, miles, of heavy copper cable from the sabotaged hydro lines, and now they were hauling the stuff to Pakistan to sell. This was no impromptu, disorganized effort. They had set up a regular salvage and shipping system: whole trains of packhorses lugged the materiel south, with stockpiles of the contraband cable in caves and huts all along the trail, awaiting transport the rest of the way to the border. Though the high-grade copper would fetch a hefty sum in Pakistan, money wasn't the main point: by refusing to be terrorized, by pilfering the enemy's treasure out from under him, the Afghans had taken back the dignity the bombs had destroyed.

These were fragile triumphs, however. The farther we went Inside, the more desperate the overall situation seemed. Everyone we met on the trail had another dire story for us. We could hear the peal of bombing from the northwest, as we passed through the town of Azrow and climbed into the barren hills beyond. It was frightening, depressing.

We were on the last leg of the journey, crossing a stretch of badlands, a sere waste of rocks, thornbrush, and exhausted soil. I was about two hundred feet out in front of the main column of men and animals; I clambered up out of the ravine we had been following. Up ahead, the trail crossed a tract of open ground before climbing another gravel-choked, boulder-strewn wadi. Suddenly, an earsplitting howl filled the air. I froze in my tracks and looked back. A moment later two MIGs streaked down the canyon, wingtip to wingtip, just fifty feet off the ground. The pilots saw me, and tilted their wings for a better look. We stared at each other for an instant that seemed to stretch on forever. Less than a hundred feet separated us. Then they straightened, flew down the canyon and disappeared, just as the caravan emerged from the shadows of the canyon floor below. If the pilots had seen the armed men and pack animals, they would have attacked and killed us all.

I was shaken, but Mister Etibari and the mujahedin only laughed. "Allah willed it," they said. "Allah wills everything." Their faith was always there, unfailing, unshakable.

Jegdeleg was proud of its tradition of resistance and rebellion. Back in the winter of 1842, during the first Anglo-Afghan war, the local tribesmen trapped an entire British army in the gorges to the north and annihilated it. Only one man, a Doctor Brydon, survived to tell the tale, riding to safety at the British outpost at Jalalabad. More than sixteen thousand British and Indian troops, their families and camp followers, died in the fighting. You could still find bits of bone, bullets, and uniform buttons inscribed VR, VICTORIA REGINA on the steep slopes below the town. The Empire never took hold in Afghanistan.

Now, Jegdeleg fought another invader, one armed with jets, helicopters, armor, rockets, and artillery. Despite all that, and the fact that the main Kabul-Jalalabad highway lay only a few miles to the north, the town was still free. Enemy forces had fought their way into the town many times, but they had never held it for long. Under their famous commander, Mohammed Anwar Khan—he had been a college professor and a coach with Afghanistan's Olympic wrestling team

before the war—the men of Jegdeleg defended
their ruined homes, and raided as far afield as
Soroobi, the outlying district of Kabul itself.

This was a place of danger, of courage, of
heroes. MIGs and MI-24 gunships buzzed the
valley constantly, but the mujahedin only laughed
at them: psychological warfare, failing miserably.
We sat in a riprap house on a mountainside and
listened to a commander from the north, one of
Anwar's allies, hammer on a single-stringed lyre
and sing extemporaneous songs of the Jihad for
four straight hours: "Afghanistan, oh holy land of
the Faithful, the godless Shurovee have come, for
no reason they have burned your beautiful gardens, they have covered your flowers with the
blood of martyrs, but we will never forsake you."
He sang of villages destroyed, of massacres, of
convoys ambushed, of young mujahedin slain, the
whole Homeric saga of the Holy War. He was a
wonderful bard and, the mujahedin told me, a
fine warrior chieftain, famous for his hit-and-run
raids on supply columns in the Kabul River
gorges.

Like Dobanday, Jegdeleg had a haunted, sad feel.
Despite the cheery bravado of the muj, you
couldn't escape the knowledge of a precious way
of life lost, gone. There was an emptiness in this
lovely green riverine valley that transcended the
bombed houses, the cratered, fallow fields. The

families, the peaceful lifeblood of the place—the old people, the women and the young—were missing, fled to the refugee camps on the plains of Pakistan. Walking along the river, beneath the ancient trees, I almost thought I heard the voices of children laughing and playing, mingled with the sad songs of the larks and the doves: the ghosts of a happy past.

We left for Pakistan on an afternoon that threatened storm; Mister Etibari, a single armed mujahed, and myself, walking south beneath cold, lowering skies. By evening, we were descending into an alluvium-choked valley. Snow began to fall, thick, heavy flakes plummeting down, erasing the hills and ridges. It was bitter cold.

   As darkness gathered we met an ancient man, sitting alone on a boulder, watching over a flock of sheep and goats. Ancient? He looked a thousand years old, the Old Man of the Mountains; he wore tattered rags, a turban that was a bundle of rags, and his whiskers hung like a spray of icicles. He introduced himself, in a quavery squeak of a voice, as "the bandit king of the Safed Koh." "I have killed many hundreds of travelers who came this way," he said, chuckling at his own whimsical humor. When our mujahed companion asked him where we might shelter for the night, he pointed to the southwest, up a crooked, narrow draw. His village was there, he said. The old village had been in the main valley below, but the Shurovee had bombed it, destroyed it. Instead of fleeing to Pakistan, the villagers had rebuilt their community in this narrow, hidden crevice in the hills: "Even the helicopters cannot find us now, by God!" the old man laughed.

We spent the night in that secret place, in an adobe room heated by a potbellied iron stove. Our host was the brother of the self-styled bandit king, a stout yeoman with a snow-white beard, a sort of Pathan Good King Wenceslas or Saint Nicholas; he was the caretaker of the village mosque, and the man in charge of welcoming mujahedin and other travelers. While his two tiny, jewel-faced daughters, in dresses that shimmered like butterfly wings, peered shyly at us from the door, giggled and whispered, he brought us bowls of thick, creamy curd, steaming cornbread, thick gray wheat bread. He smiled upon us benevolently as we ate.

According to Mister Etibari, the original village had been destroyed by the Communists because the people had insisted on offering food and shelter to passing resistance fighters. Now, despite the community's new location, the Afghan government knew the villagers had not changed their ways, and was threatening to attack them again. When Etibari had asked our host about it, he had replied with a quotation from the Koran: "Those who believe enough to leave their homes and fight for the cause of Allah, and those who give them shelter and assistance, they are truly brothers."

The wind and snow beat against the door, and somewhere out there in the night the airborne commandos hunted; but in that poor room, in that precarious village, faith made a kind of momentary shelter.

*t*he war took over my life, filled up the years. The intervals between trips seemed less and less important, less and less real, as time went by. A friend of mine who shot combat footage for CBS put it this way: "When you go up into those mountains with those people, you leave a piece of your soul up there, and you have to go back and find yourself from time to time." Something like that: Inside was where I really lived.

Every few months I would buy another bootleg ticket on PIA, Pakistan International Airlines, round trip from New York to Islamabad. The official price was fourteen hundred and change, but my East Indian travel agent in Manhattan charged just over nine; I didn't ask. I was constantly hustling another assignment, from anyone who would help pay my way over and back before and after the fact: *Time, Mother Jones*, NPR, the Hearst papers, you name it. For a while, I even hauled a video camera into the war and shot bang-bang footage on spec for the networks. Sometimes I made money on the trips, sometimes I lost, but it didn't matter. This was what I wanted to do, what I had to do: duty and desire, rolled into one.

The flight over and back remained a small adventure in and of itself. PIA often juggled routes at the last moment without warning to maximize passenger loads. I recall one "direct nonstop" Islamabad–London–New York flight that meandered from Islamabad south to Karachi, lingered there awhile, then wandered up through the Persian Gulf, stopped off in Damascus, and finally continued on to Heathrow and New York. The weather on the impromptu route was horrible, and we spent the extra six or eight hours' flying time wallowing and lurching through sickening zero-visibility turbulence. And there was always the threat of terrorism. One man was arrested at Islamabad International Airport the night before I flew home trying to board the London–New York flight with a briefcase that contained a folding-stock Kalashnikov assault rifle, three ammo clips, and four hand grenades. He evidently hadn't heard of luggage X-ray machines. After the police beat him for several hours, he confessed that he had planned to mow down the other passengers as they boarded, in the name of Palestinian Solidarity, More Rights for Shiites, something like that.

The leg of the journey inside Pakistan was even more interesting. The old Fokker prop plane

that flew from Islamabad to Peshawar had a left
engine that regularly caught on fire; you could
watch it spout flames and smoke from takeoff to
landing, for a solid hour. When the flight finally
went down with all hands one day, though, it
wasn't because of engine failure. Coming in for a
landing in Peshawar, it flew over a Pathan wed-
ding celebration, where the guests, as was cus-
tomary, were firing guns in the air to salute the
bride and groom. The celebrants weren't watching
where they were shooting, and several streams of
Kalashnikov fire hit the plane. All of the forty-odd
people on board died in the ensuing crash.

The journeys from Peshawar across the Tribal
Area to the border remained as wild as ever. I got
arrested by the Pakistani Army and police so
many times out there I lost count. Luckily, I
always managed to talk my way out of going to
jail. My old photographer friend Ed Grazda had
worse luck, after two dope-smoking Frontier Con-
stabulary plainclothesmen arrested him on his
way back into Pakistan, above Terri Mangal.
"They took me to the police station in Parachinar, which was pure hell," he recalled later.
"When I yelled for them to call the American
embassy, they shackled me to a post out front.
Then they brought in a local tribesman who
needed to be shackled more than I did, because
he had just murdered somebody, so they took the
shackles off me and put them on him—they only
had one set of manacles and chains. By the time

they let me go two days later I had incredible bug bites and blisters, plus a urinary tract infection and giardiasis." It was all part of the scene, the Afghan experience.

Inside, it was the best of times, it was the worst and most wasted of times, and even after half a dozen trips a lifetime long it was the strangest of times and places. War accelerated events to unbearable, impossible speeds—no neat rites of passage to wisdom or peace here but runaway craziness rushing into yet crazier craziness. Sometimes it seemed like one long, endlessly long journey through a war that would never end.

We are in the high mountains west of the Swat Valley, east of the Kunar, with a band of merry muj straight out of Robin Hood. We cross gleaming summits, by waterfalls, heaps of snow debouched by avalanche chutes. The people here live in log cabins in the forest; one man and his wife have adopted seven war orphans from all across Afghanistan, a rainbow coalition of tribes and races. The kids play in the sunny pine needles by the front door. An RPG-7 grenade launcher and an AK-47 hang over the mantle.

The muj have a Chinese BM-12 multitube rocket launcher hidden in the evergreens overlooking the enemy fire base at Barikot. We spend a morning lobbing rockets inside the perimeter fortifications; the next day, we continue the barrage with an Oerlikon gun dug in even closer to Barikot. When the Soviets reply with heavy mortar fire, the muj gun crews take shelter in dugouts and caves, and the rest of us retreat down the opposite side of the mountain, away from the enemy. The mortar shells keep screaming down as we descend across the blond meadows, the sunburnt timber, through the long afternoon. The fire is surprisingly accurate; perhaps the Soviets have a spotter, a forward observer with a radio, hiding somewhere on the mountains above. I have never known a lovelier afternoon; it must be the nearness, the possibility, of death, sweetening the golden light, the smell of the mountain grass, the laughter of the mujahedin as more shells whistle down wide of the mark and explode, black columns of smoke rising into the evening sky . . .

We are leaving a teahouse in the western Safed Koh, near Kabul, when a tough-looking band of muj arrives. They are covered with dust, and you can almost smell the high explosives on them; they clank with grenades, ammo clips, assault rifles, carbines and bayonets, and they have that weary swagger which says they are fresh from the battlefield, from combat.

The commander is a barrel-chested little man with a kaffiyeh knotted around his neck, his Chitrali cap pushed over to one side like a beret. When he recognizes me as a foreign journalist, he

is excited. He begins talking to me in French, and
then, when I tell him I am American, he switches
to English. "I was a teacher before the war," he
tells me. Now, you see what I do," he says,
smiling regretfully, gesturing at his Kalashnikov
and ammo vest.

He tells me he and his men are from Paghman, north of Kabul. "You must come there!" he
says. "There is fighting there all day, every day—
not like anyplace else in Afghanistan." Like many
Afghans, he has the gift of being proud of the
looniest things. "The Shurovee and the Communists use everything in Paghman—MIGs,
Sukhois, helicopters, T-62 tanks, T-72 tanks,
BM-12 rockets, BM-40 rockets, gas . . ." He
sounds like a pitchman for the Seven Circles of
Hell Chamber of Commerce. Before we part, he
reaches into an inside pocket and produces, of all
things, a business card, which he hands to me:

MOHAMMED ACHMEDZAI
COMMANDANT LOGAR-KABUL

with a post office box in Peshawar, and a space for
a phone number, blank.

A few months later, when I am in Peshawar
again, I write him a note, but I never receive a
reply. A year or two after that, someone who has
just come from Paghman tells me he thinks the
little commander is dead: "Just about all the
hard-core muj near the highway are dead by now.

All the villages are gone. There's nobody left." I don't know.

We enter an area that has just been—what? Erased, liquidated, annihilated. First bombing, then a convoy sweep, then more bombing, and choppers working over the rubble. You can still smell the sweet odor of the dead, deep in the ruins, in the craters.

The mujahedin stop to pray, and I wander off behind a row of gutted houses, to look around. I don't know why. It is dawn, and a day moon is rising over the hills.

I am standing at the edge of a field when I see the madman: a big, shambling figure, walking beneath the trees at the field's far end. There is something wrong, deranged, about his movements. Then he sees me, and a look of twisted delight appears on his face. "*Shurovee!*" he cries. "*Shurovee!*" He breaks a limb off one of the trees and runs across the field toward me.

Does he actually think I am a Russian, dropped from the sky for him to kill? Or does he think at all? No one else is left alive here; everyone else is dead, or gone. Why stay on here, unless you are mad? Or maybe he has been digging in the ruins for his wife, his children.

As he reaches me, and I see in his eyes just how crazy he is, I finally realize how much danger I am in. I call out to the mujahedin and back up against the wall. He stops, and begins beating the tree limb on the ground, breaking off the leaves and twigs, trimming it into a proper club. He may be a homicidal maniac, but he is a damnably efficient one. Luckily, my friends round the corner just in time. They disarm the madman and tell him I am not a Russian, I am a friend of the Jihad. "He has come here to help us."

But the madman has the last word, as he should; after all this is a war, and nothing is going to put his village, his life, together again. As he stomps away, he turns and glares at me with those toxic eyes, and growls, "I don't care. I'd like to kill him anyway."

seven

985, 1986, sliding into 1987: looking back on it, these were the darkest and most paradoxically black-magical years of the war. Underarmed, out of ammunition, disorganized and hungry, the mujahedin crawled from the ruins of their villages and fought on. Lacking proper weapons, a real plan, the ghost of a logical chance, the Jihad ran on heroes and myths. Even when they were killed, executed and buried in a mass grave or blown away into nothingness by a bomb, the saints and heroes never completely died; they came sneaking back in songs and stories that sent another hundred out to emulate those who had gone before.

One of the first, before my time in the war, was the big ex-policeman who led an urban guerrilla outfit in Kabul in the early days of the Soviet occupation. Tales described him as a towering figure with an even mightier voice, a voice that, along with his mad courage, was a kind of mujahedin secret weapon. He would begin night attacks on Soviet and Afghan government positions by shouting *"Allaho akbar!"* into a bullhorn, and then shouting for the enemy to surrender to the soldiers of Allah. According to the stories, whole Afghan Army garrisons came over to the resistance side at his words, the power of his speech, and corps of infidel invaders fled before the first shots were fired. But one night he stood up with his bullhorn, ready to begin another attack, and someone on the other side fired blindly into the darkness and hit him right between the eyes.

Another legendary character was the young RPG-7 gunner from Wardak Province, west of Kabul. A student before the Soviet invasion, he had become a self-taught genius in the arcane craft of antitank rocketry. In four years, he had knocked out a dozen tanks, armored personnel carriers, and infantry fighting machines, and scores of supply trucks and fuel tankers. There were pictures of him everywhere, in refugee camps and resistance offices in Pakistan, on farmhouse and *chaikhanna* walls in Afghanistan: a slender, ascetic, hawk-boned youth with wistful determined eyes, wearing the leather tank crewman's helmet taken from one of his dead victims. He too died at the peak of his fame: one too many tanks taken on at close quarters, a rocket-propelled grenade with a dud warhead (or perhaps he was too close to his target: the RPG-7 has to travel a certain distance before it arms), and a burst of counterfire . . . He died before he could get off another shot.

And, among all the rest, Brigadier Afghani. The Soviets finally trapped him and killed him at his base in Tirzeen, shortly after I returned from that wintry crossing of the Safed Koh. MIGs and gunships blasted the area for days, and then copterborne commandos landed to the south, a blocking force for a column of tanks and regular infantry from the north. Like all the other dead, Brigadier Afghani and his men went down fighting. When I came back to the Safed Koh a year and a half later, people talked about him, his charisma, his courage, his raffish contempt for the enemy, as if he were still alive, and there were still mujahedin at Tirzeen.

Even tragedies and defeats were turned by a kind of tribal magic into power. I visited a nomad camp in the brown foothills above Logar on one of my first treks into the war zone, and the people there told me this story. Another band of their tribe was camped above Kabul a few months back; some of the men went down to the city to sell animals in the bazaar. They were gone for two days. On the first morning, two Russian MI-24 helicopters cruised by, looking for guerrillas. They passed the camp, the herds, and then suddenly they curved back, and attacked. They fired their .57-mm rockets, their Gatling guns; they dropped their high-explosive bombs. It took less than thirty seconds for them to destroy the tents and kill most of the herd animals and many of the people. Then they flew away.

Among the dead was the young bride of the tribal khan's oldest son; they had only been married a few months. When the young man returned from Kabul and found his wife had been killed, he went to her grave, sat down on the heaped stones, and shot himself with his rifle, the rough old-fashioned carbine that Afghan men carry to protect their families and herds against wolves and bandits. When they told the story, the nomads seemed to be saying, "Even our deaths are more beautiful, truer, than the lives of the enemy, the invader who believes in nothing."

The stories they told turned metaphysics upside down, logic as we know it inside out. An aristocratic young Afghan friend of mine, educated, well traveled, told me the Shurovee, the unbelievers, could never conquer holy Afghanistan. Why, up north, even the snakes were fighting against the Soviets. In one valley, all the poisonous serpents had met and agreed not to bite any loyal Afghans until the war was over; but when a Soviet patrol tried to enter the valley, the troopers were met by a phalanx of hissing, writhing warrior-snakes, and they had to flee. How could Afghanistan ever be defeated, with defenders like these?

There was one kind of yarn some of us who covered the war called "too good to be true" stories. There were many variations, but generally they went like this. A lone guerrilla armed with an old RPG-7 is passing a big Soviet base in the evening, and he looks and happens to see a fuel truck parked near the perimeter wire. More on a whim than anything else, he aims his grenade launcher and fires, scoring a direct hit. The truck brews up and burns, and then, as the exultant mujahed watches, the fire spreads to a gasoline storage tank complex nearby. The fire explodes a thousandfold, defying the efforts of the Soviets to put it out, and a few minutes later it sets off the base's main armory and ammo dump: the whole place goes up in a cataclysmic series of secondary and tertiary explosions, destroying 417 armored vehicles and 563 trucks, and killing 3,923 Soviet soldiers and officers. (The figures were always scrupulously exact in these fabulous tales.) I must have heard one or another version of that one a dozen times, at least.

In another, even more exquisite twist of the tale, the Soviets themselves triggered their own doom. A Soviet officer spies a lone guerrilla, or shepherd, or farmer, on a hill nearby, and he orders a truck-mounted BM-40 rocket battery to open fire; the intended victim goes unscathed, of course, as the rocket inevitably goes astray, hits a fuel depot, which catches fire and sets off a row of ammunition bunkers . . .

Of course these stories were funny, but they

also contained a certain secret truth, as elusive and durable as the mujahedin themselves were and the Shurovee were not.

You ended up with so many stories, firsthand and secondhand, that you just couldn't handle them anymore; the war accelerated reality to unbearable speeds that blew your mind, burned out your sensibilities, and constantly threatened to break your heart. The only way to deal with it was to try and forget what you couldn't afford to remember, and style the rest for laughs if you could. Like the way Gunston told of the death of a guerrilla commander he knew and liked: "Raheem was a nice young chap," he used to say, grinning, "till he got careless and dropped two shells down a mortar at the same time." What else could you say?

I remember getting a letter from a photographer friend, posted in Pakistan after his fifth or sixth trip to the war zone. It began, "I have so many horror stories about Afghanistan that I can't remember them all," and it went on from there into a wild series of black tales . . . A party of muj from Jegdeleg walked into a stay-behind ambush by Soviet Spetsnaz commandos and were wiped out; a commander gave up, sold his antiaircraft guns on the black market in Pakistan, and used the money to go on the pilgrimage to Mecca. And it finished up with a classic that anyone who had been in Afghanistan, in peace or war, could in-

stantly click with: "Muj comes into a teahouse in
Paktia with an unexploded cluster bomb. Borrows
Swiss Army knife from a journalist, starts trying to
open bomb to see what's inside. Journalists tell
him stop, but he won't. Journalists leave. Minute
later teahouse explodes, three dead, four wounded, people screaming. Journalists bandage
wounded and leave . . ." At the time, just back
from Afghanistan myself, I thought it was one of
the funniest stories I had ever heard. If the
Afghans survived through myths, perhaps we survived through jokes. You did what you had to do.

Then there were the videos of the war we watched
every weekend on the VCR at the British Afghanaid offices out in University Town. The Brits had
collected a whole library of Afghan War footage,
and new tapes were always being brought in by
journalists returning from the battlefields. Correspondents, mujahedin, French doctors, aid workers, and hangers-on crouched in front of the
screen for hours, as if no one could get enough of
those dreadful images: corpses in a ditch, villages
going up in smoke, refugees with blank, wasted
faces, helicopter gunships hunting through awful
skies . . . One tape, which we called "the bombing tape," just showed bombs, big ones, two-
thousand-pounders, exploding across fields and
orchards for endless minutes that seemed like
hours: in some ways, with its combination of

horror, inexorable destruction, and ultimate utter meaninglessness, it seemed the perfect icon of modern war.

A cruelly comic favorite among the journalists was the tape of a film shot by an unfortunate Australian stringer up in Paktia Province the year before. Its final sequence showed a tank rolling toward the camera, closer and closer, and then confusion and tumbling darkness. According to the story, the cameraman had set up to film a captured Soviet T-62 tank, a dramatic head-on sequence. The muj who volunteered to drive the thing swore he knew how—"Yes, they taught me before I deserted from the Afghan Army." But when the tank started moving toward the cameraman, it just kept accelerating, and the unfortunate filmmaker, peering intently through his viewfinder and trying to frame and focus, didn't notice. The tank just kept coming, faster and faster, till it rolled right over the cameraman, crushing him beneath its treads, but knocking the camera and its film aside. The victim died several agonizing minutes later, according to embarrassed muj who were on the scene. When you heard everyone (including yourself) whooping with laughter as the screen faded to black, you prayed that when, if, you died in the war at least you wouldn't go out in a pratfall.

For their part, the Afghans at the party had one tape they never tired of seeing, even if they already knew it by heart. Shot by a daring young

Polish-English photographer named Andy (he would be killed a few years later in Nuristan, by bandits or renegade muj), it showed a daring daylight ambush on the Salang Highway, the main Soviet supply line north of Kabul. The tape began with a long panoramic shot of the road, with a column of trucks and armored vehicles descending a gorge. Guerrillas gathered in the brush below the highway embankment. The attack began when a mujahed fired a rocket-propelled grenade point-blank into the turret of a passing tank. The turret spewed smoke, and a burly crewman popped out of the hatch, was hit by small-arms fire, fell, slid down the embankment, and expired messily at the cameraman's feet.

When the attack ended, the entire convoy was destroyed; the road was filled with stalled and burning vehicles, sprawled corpses, pools of oil, debris. Guerrillas moved through the wreckage, picking up weapons, torching trucks and armor. Watching the Afghans watch the tape, you could see it was a kind of talisman to them, their myth made flesh. Looking at their slain enemies, the ruins of the war machine, they could believe in themselves once more.

eight

he Afghans stole the power from the most sacred and lethal of their enemy's artifacts and ways. There was the story of the helicopter, shot down by mujahedin along the approaches to the Panjshir Valley. They moved the fuselage next to a trail and set up an ice cream parlor in it, using snow from a nearby glacier and fruit syrups to make the stuff. It was good marketing: there was a special joy for war-weary muj in sipping sherbet in the carcass of the airborne dragon that had terrorized them. Later, when business along the trail dwindled, someone put wheels on the chopper and an old truck engine in it, and when last heard from, the Soviet helicopter was hauling passengers as a minibus on the Charikot road.

That was no isolated instance; it was a full-blown syndrome. South of Jalalabad, I was talking to a tough-looking commander when he reached casually inside his jacket and pulled out a Soviet butterfly mine. I jumped back instinctively, and

the rogue chuckled to himself as he cracked the
evil device with his fingers, opened a cunningly
hinged lid, scooped out a load of *naswar*, the
potent green snuff of the Afghans, and stashed it
under his lower lip. It was a great act: *They tried
to kill me with this thing; I took it and turned it
into a snuffbox. What do you think about that,
huh?*

One time, my photographer friend Ed Grazda
visited a village that had been raided recently
by Soviet airborne commandos. As they fought
the villagers, the Soviets had used RPG-22
rocket launchers to blast through walls and doors.
When they departed, they left the disposable
tubular launchers behind. After the villagers rebuilt their adobe-walled houses, they used these
deadly objects to beautify the community,
sticking them upright along both sides of the
main street and planting trees and flowers in
them.

In the Safed Koh Mountains, we stopped for
the night in yet another gutted, ripped-out town,
bomb craters everywhere, the houses abandoned.
It had been destroyed by repeated helicopter and
jet attacks. One of the mujahedin was from the
town; he lived with his family in a refugee camp in
Pakistan now, traveling back to Afghanistan periodically to fight. He led us inside his house;
it had been damaged by bombing, holes in the
charred walls, roof buckling over broken beams,
but he was still proud of it. He showed us through

the big rooms, pointing to the bread ovens, the carved wooden doors . . .

On one wall was a mural, painted in pastel shades of green, red, blue, and yellow. It showed a tree, the tree of life; the leafy branches were filled with delicate little singing birds. Above the tree, the artist had painted a Soviet MI-24 helicopter gunship. It hovered there, its gun spitting bullets, iron bombs tumbling from its belly. The artist had imbued the deadly machine with the same grace and energy as the tree, the birds. The man who owned the house—had he painted the scene himself?—smiled at me proudly. From the dirt and straw of the floor to the beams and thatch of the ceiling, a mysterious power seemed to fill the room.

nine

eyond everything else, you were hit with terror, bitterness, injustice, much too much to handle. If you let it get to you, it could kill you; if you didn't, you were so numb you might as well be dead.

A British woman named Rainey used to tell the following story; she told it again and again, as if she were spitting out more of the poison every time. It didn't work, of course, but it was something we all did; if there wasn't anyone else to talk to, you just told your stories to yourself.

She was hiding in a blown-up farmhouse near Gardez. The mujahedin had ambushed a government convoy on the plains below and had pinned it down, and helicopter gunships were trying to break it loose. Teams of choppers would come in, bomb and rocket and shoot till they ran out of ammo, and fly back to Kabul to refuel and rearm and then return to the attack.

This went on in the distance, miles away, and just outside the farmhouse, a little boy watched

over a herd of sheep and goats. Then, toward
evening, one of the helicopters peeled away from
the battle and flew their way. It stopped above,
and hovered, as if deciding what to do. Then the
nosegun brayed; the ground outside vanished in
shrouds of dust and smoke, and when it cleared
the boy and his animals were dead, shot to bloody
pieces. The MI-24 hung there a moment longer,
as if admiring its handiwork, and then it flew
away.

There were a million victims, with a million stories. You had to listen to them, didn't you? After
all, that was why you were there.

She was still beautiful, but through the
beauty you could see what they had done to her. A
lightning streak of white sliced through her jet-
black hair, and when she stopped talking you
could see her eyes drift away and the memories,
the fear, and the hurt take over. Your heart went
out to her, you feared for her.

She had been a schoolteacher in Kabul, a
quiet, gentle woman; when the Communists took
over and the Soviets invaded to help them, her
indignation got the best of her and she joined the
resistance. The group she belonged to were hardly
firebrands: they printed and distributed the anon-
ymous insurgent broadsheets called *shabhanama*,
"night letters," and they helped organize protest
marches and demonstrations. Then someone

informed on her; KGB and KHAD agents came to her house at night and took her away. She was beaten, tortured with acid and electrical shock. Finally, her captors locked her in The Room.

"It was dark, so dark I couldn't see," she said. "There was a terrible smell, of blood, decay, death. Slowly, my eyes adjusted to the darkness, and then I began to see. All around me were *pieces of women*—piles of legs, of breasts, of arms, torsos, heads. There was blood everywhere, on the walls, the ceiling, the floor. There was a drain in the center of the floor, or the room would have been flooded with blood."

She began to sob. "I looked at one of the faces. It was a woman I knew, one of my friends from school . . ."

The bitterness cut both ways, of course.

My friend was from Kandahar; he had been a mujahed until a Kalashnikov round put a dent in the side of his skull. Now he ran a shop in an alleyway behind Green's Hotel, off Saddar Road in Peshawar, selling Afghan carpets and clothing and captured Soviet uniforms and equipment.

This morning, he was rifling the drawers and shelves in his shop, searching furiously for some photographs he wanted to show me. "Very good peectures! Commander, he cut off head"—he chopped at his own sinewy neck for emphasis—

"from one hundred Communist, he take peecture one hundred Communist head—" But the photos were nowhere to be found. I wasn't that surprised, I was used by now to his strange enthusiasms and moods; the bullet that dinged his cranium seemed to have knocked some of the equilibrium out of it as well. Then he launched into the story of the Frenchman and the soup:

"This same commander—he good, good commander!—he shoot down MIG, he catch Russian pilot, he cut him up into big pot, he make soup. He have big cave in mountain, he eating soup in cave. French doctor come Kandahar, he look to build clinic, he come mountain, he visit cave. Commander tell him, 'Welcome Afghanistan.' He sit down with commander, commander give him soup. Doctor eating soup, he like soup too much, he say, 'This good soup. What this soup?' Commander, he smile. He take top off pot, he put in hand, he take out pilot head—" He mimicked the commander holding high the severed, boiled head. "Doctor, he very, very angry! He leave cave, he leave Kandahar, he say he never come Afghanistan again." He paused, smiling fondly at the tale. "Commander, he *good, good* commander," he concluded.

I never really decided whether the story was true or not, although there was no doubt about it, my friend believed it. In his mind, it was so good it had to be true. What did you expect, in a

country, a war, where the innocent dead num-
bered anywhere from five hundred thousand to
two million, maybe more—no one in the world
knew because no one in the world bloody cared? I
had my moments when I hated with the best, or
worst, of them, and it wasn't even really my war.

ten

The ranges of the Khyber Pass rose in towering, forbidding ranks, barren slopes glinting like steel in the hot sun. You irresistibly thought of Eliot: "Dead mountain mouth of carious teeth that cannot spit" . . . "Voices singing out of empty cisterns and exhausted wells . . ." Wasteland. The trail ran through gorges as narrow as a broom closet, through perilous notches where armed tribesmen, Zakhakhels and Kukikhels, pondered your passing with feral flinty eyes. Wasteland, bandit country, no-man's-zone.

On the Jihad road again. We were bound from the Khyber to Jalalabad, the back way, the same route the British had taken when they tried to subdue the Zakhakhels in the last century; they failed, and you could see why. A single sniper could have held up an entire army for hours in those winding chasms, on those impassable walls.

The trip was my idea, and I had persuaded Ed Grazda to come along. He hadn't been Inside since a bombing raid had nearly killed him two years ago in Jegdeleg; the bombs had bounced him three feet off the ground, and a group of pack mules twenty feet away were chopped to pieces by shrapnel. Understandably, he was still gun-shy, but I had persuaded him that this would be a relatively easy trip. Before it was over, he would be cursing me and the day he listened to me.

We were traveling with a party of guerrilla reinforcements from the refugee camps, led by a solemn-faced mullah, an Islamic scholar who was also a commander. He carried a Kalashnikov and a well-thumbed volume of the Holy Koran. Every time we stopped for tea, he gobbled down handfuls of antidepressant pills, the kind you are supposed to take four times a day if you have been seriously contemplating suicide; he was putting away twenty at a time. Who could blame him? In Afghanistan in 1987 there were plenty of reasons for the blues.

It took us till evening to cross the mountain rampart south of the Khyber; the next day, we set out across the Tirah Valley. This was the heartland of the Zakhakhel country, and it lay completely outside the control of the Pakistani government; there were no roads, no police posts, no soldiers. The tribesmen did whatever they wanted, which generally ranged from banditry and smuggling to high crime and insurrection. The valley floor was a sea of opium poppies, mile after mile of shimmering red, white, and blue

flowers, pods the size of billiard balls; the raw sap
went to make heroin in labs on the Khyber and in
Soviet-occupied Jalalabad. Throughout most of
the war, the Zakhakhels had been taking arms
and money from the Soviets and the Kabul government in return for fighting against the mujahedin and the government of Pakistan. Not that they
needed much urging: the Zakhakhels loved to
fight.

Luckily, the mujahedin had recently cobbled
together an uneasy peace with the Zakhakhels. As
we trudged through the fields of blossoming nar-
cotic, past fortified mud-walled towns, people
greeted us warmly; they asked us how the Holy
War was going around Jalalabad, what was
happening in Peshawar, and what those accursed
Kukikhels to the north were up to . . . the vital
gossip of the trail. Still, you suspected those
smiles could vanish in an instant, and the guns
come out. You kept your eyes open.

That afternoon, we left the Tirah and began
climbing into the mountains to the west. By evening, we reached Morro, a resistance camp of
tents and tunnels on a pass straddling the frontier.
Beyond, more tumbled summits of stone and dust
led away into Afghanistan, separated by yawning
gorges. It looked like the edge of the world, the
land of the lost, but some of the bloodiest fighting

in the war had gone on down there, over control of the vital border passes and infiltration routes.

The commander at Morro was a jaunty old peasant who bore a passing resemblance to the cartoon character Yosemite Sam. He had lost one leg above the knee to a Soviet bomb; his artificial limb was a creaky, clumsy contraption of iron and wood. He complained that it kept him from going on raids against the enemy anymore, and he asked if I could find him something better back in Peshawar; he had heard the Red Cross had good ones. "By God, give me a new leg and I'll kick the Shurovee all the way to Moscow!" he exclaimed.

I liked the old man, and I promised him I would do what I could, though we both knew promises were hard to keep in wartime Afghanistan; people were swept away from you, never to be seen again, and love and mercy were scattered away on the winds and lost.

The journey took two more days: down the canyon of the Nazian River, along the edge of the Kabul River valley, and back up into the mountains south of Jalalabad. Hard traveling. I blistered and soaked my feet the first morning, fording the Nazian, and as we slogged on the raw water-logged flesh rubbed, ripped apart, disintegrated, till I could barely walk. The country down on

the plains was disquieting: the nearest enemy
fire bases were only three or four miles from the
trail—you could see the bunkers and barbed
wire clearly—and the villages were not friendly.
They had pledged fealty to both the Kabul
regime, to avoid being bombed, and the Jihad,
and our mujahedin companions didn't trust
them.

Recently, guerrillas from the mountains had
assassinated many Communist sympathizers and
collaborators in the area, the mullah said, and
they should have killed more. These were bad
people; if they were good, among the righteous,
then why hadn't the Shurovee bombed their villages? It was a relief, when we finally turned back
up another valley, up into the unequivocal freedom of the mountains.

The last afternoon, as we left a village teahouse
high in the canyon on our final march to the
guerrilla base, we heard the buzz of jets. Someone
pointed, and we saw them: a host of predatory
specks, circling a stony ridge in the distance
above us. Bombs were exploding, one after another; we saw the gray plumes of smoke, and a few
moments later the faint thunderous sounds
reached us. Soon the ridge top vanished beneath a
thick pall.

"What's the name of that place?" I asked.

"Speena Bora," one of the guerrillas replied.

It sounded suspiciously familiar. I thought for a second; then I decided to ask. "What's the name of the *marcaz* where we're going?"

"Speena Bora," the muj said. We headed on up the trail.

eleven

*t*here I was, standing on that same ridge-line, waiting for more bombs to fall, my camera in my hand.

I was surrounded by mujahedin, the group I had come to call "the Hilltop Boys." Whenever the MIGs came to bombard Speena Bora, which happened six, eight, a dozen times a day, everyone who wasn't manning antiaircraft guns on the mountains crowded into the air raid tunnels. But these characters, there were maybe fifteen or twenty of them, were different: they raced to the summit of the ridge and stood there defiantly, firing rifles, AKs, and RPGs at the impossibly high jets, shouting taunts at the enemy and praises to Allah as the bombs went off all around them. When I asked them if it was very dangerous, if anyone was ever killed, they said, "Oh yes."

We had been at the marcaz a week when I finally decided to go up there with them. It had been a nasty seven days. The guerrilla offensive on Jalalabad had broken down, and now the enemy was counterattacking everywhere; the way beyond Speena Bora was blocked. Nasty days, crouching in a tunnel as the bombs fell, listening to the reports from the front grow worse and worse . . . waiting, waiting, waiting, for something to come that you didn't want to come. For me, going up on the ridge was less an act of courage than of absolute, mindless desperation.

It was nearly eight A.M.; the first air raid of the day was long overdue. I looked north from the ridge, out over a landscape of vast and awesome desolation. Steep mountainsides pitched away to dry river and creek beds far below, more sawtooth ridges beyond, a tumult of dusty hills; beyond the faded green valley of the Kabul River, more mountains, range on range, marched away to the horizon, the highest summits blanched with snow. The only vegetation was the parched thorny brush, gnawed down by centuries of famished sheep and goats.

To the Afghans this was Holy Land, worth bleeding and dying over for a thousand years to keep sanctified, pure. It was threadbare, maniacally crumpled, and dry as a bone. There were two elderly hermits living near the marcaz, surviving off the generosity of the mujahedin: skinny little men, half blind, with long, wispy whiskers. When they washed before praying, as all Muslims do, they used handfuls of dust; water was far too scarce. I really didn't want to die there.

Perhaps nothing would happen today, I thought; perhaps the Soviets would take the day off. It was already past eight-thirty, and the skies to the west were empty still. The mujahedin sat around me on the rocks, talking and joking, cleaning their weapons. Sunlight gleamed on the frozen slopes of the Safed Koh to the south. A bird whistled in the gorge below.

Like the other air raids, this one began with the hard stammer of heavy machine guns on the peaks to the west, as the guerrillas there sighted the approaching planes and opened fire on them. A few moments later we heard the drone of the jets, and then we could see them. The man next to me grabbed my shoulder and pointed and there they were, three pairs of specks that quickly grew into shining metal darts. The mujahedin were standing, shouting "*Allaho akbar!*" and "*Shurovee mordabad,*" "Death to the Russians."

Then the MIGs were circling above us. Everyone around me began shooting. An explosion behind me nearly tore my eardrums out; I turned and saw a guerrilla holding a smoking grenade launcher. According to the muj, the enemy pilots often mistook the exhaust trails from RPGs for Stinger or SAM-7 antiaircraft missiles, and panicked and fled when they saw them; it was a good way to drive the Shurovee jets away. Not this time, though; the MIGs continued to circle above us, acquiring targets, zeroing in for the kill.

It was total madness. A dozen muj were blazing away with Kalashnikovs and Enfields; the air was filled with the reek of cordite, rainbows of spent brass clattering onto the ridge. The insane yowl of the jet engines, the heavy machine guns hammering away from the mountains, the shouting, more explosions as more rocket-propelled grenades were fired . . . There was almost too much sound and fury to think, to be afraid, but I managed both. There was no way the Hilltop Boys were going to bring down a MIG, or even harass them—their bullets were falling thousands and thousands of feet short—but I understood why they did it. Once you started flinching, cowering, it was hard to stop; you had to stand out there and face down the Juggernaut in a war as unequal as this one. That kind of extreme behavior was a mujahedin secret weapon, one of the main reasons they were winning the war, or at least not losing it. If the Soviets bombed this ridgeline for a millennium, there would still be partisans standing there, firing at them and crying out their defiance and their faith at the end of it all.

I was terrified, but I managed to keep my wits about me enough to keep filming with the heavy Beta videocamera, tracking the jets as they swooped down on their bombing runs, pulling back to focus on an exultant muj ten feet away ripping away with his AK on full automatic . . . Again, the sensory overload of it all helped to take the edge off the fear, giving it no time or room to operate.

The MIGs made their runs, and suddenly the commander who looked like an Old Testament prophet, who had carried the huge volume of the Koran in with him from Pakistan, grabbed my arm and pulled me down next to him in a crouch. A moment later the bombs were going off all around us, greasy fireballs of napalm taller than houses. If the MIGs had dropped cluster bombs, or even simple high explosive, we would have been killed. The flames drifted away, down the mountainsides. We watched as the MIGs wheeled back toward the west. One of them was trailing smoke from a wing, flying slower than the rest. The guns on the mountains must have scored a hit. War whoops echoed down the ridge.

It was all over, I realized suddenly; and I was still alive. The camera was still on, dangling at the end of my limp arm, filming a documentary of my boots in the dust. When I tried to switch it off, my fingers began to tremble uncontrollably. I felt a smile form on my lips, and I looked over at the commander, and he was smiling, too, smiling back at me. I could smell the raw petrol incense of the napalm, rising from where the bombs had impacted. We might be dead tomorrow, but no one could steal this wild moment of triumph from us, ever.

Two days later, Grazda and I decided to leave. There were just too many signs to ignore;

when the muj had begun digging holes and bury-
ing their ammunition and heavy weapons the
evening before, that was the clincher. It looked
like the Sovs were breaking through and the guerrillas were preparing to abandon the place, and
that wasn't a story I wanted to cover.

We wanted to leave very early in the morning,
before the bombing began again, but we ran afoul
of the Afghans' incredibly inappropriate sense of
humor. Divining our anxiousness to leave, the
young commander who seemed to be in charge
insisted we sit with him on the open bomb-
cratered mountainside while he drafted a letter of
passage to accompany us. He made a great show
of mulling interminably over the wording, then
penning a few words painstakingly, then cogitat-
ing again. It drove Grazda to distraction; he was
weary of the bombing, and he really, really
wanted to be gone. He fidgeted and cursed aloud,
and the madder he got, of course, the longer the
commander dawdled, out of sheer Afghan orneri-
ness. The sun was climbing high in the sky now; I
expected to hear the ugly buzz of MIGs at any
moment. At last, the scrivener came to the bottom
of the page. He signed the letter with a flourish,
and Grazda let out an audible sigh of relief:
"About fucking time!"

But our tormentor wasn't through. He started
to fold the paper, then pantomimed a double take,
turned the page over, and began writing on the
other side: a postscript, thanking one of the com-

manders down the trail for the loan of some antitank rockets a few months back. I thought Grazda
was going to spontaneously combust, go up in
flames right there on the mountainside. Actually,
it was pretty funny.

At long last the letter was completed, and it
was time to go. We hugged the muj and wished
them well. They were standing on dangerous
ground, and we didn't know if we would ever see
them again. In wartime Afghanistan, goodbye
usually meant goodbye forever. We set off down
the trail toward Pakistan.

We were resting at a muj teahouse an hour and a
half later when things began to happen. We heard
the roar of planes, much too loud, and we ran
outside in time to see a MIG scream overhead,
low; it was popping parachute flares to decoy
heat-seeking missiles, and it was heading east,
the same direction we were. More MIGs followed;
their bomb racks were full, and the red stars on
the fuselage blazed in the sunlight. Somebody was
going to catch hell; maybe us.

A few minutes later the local commander
arrived. We had to leave immediately, he said:
the Shurovee were coming up the valley with
masses of tanks and infantry, and more enemy
troops were said to be moving to block the trail up
ahead. The fighting was going to be very, very

bad. He couldn't spare any of his men to accompany us, but there were two farmers he knew, on
their way to the border with packhorses, and we
could go with them. They were good, honorable
men. If we made it to Pakistan, he added seriously, we should pay the men one thousand afghanis
each, a total of about twenty-four U.S. dollars.
Not a penny more, he warned: one thousand afs
was the proper, the fair, price.

It was pure, panicked flight. Basically, Ed
and I threw our gear onto the horses and fled for
our lives, accompanied by the two farmers. There
was no thought of dignity or honor, only shame-
less survival.

We were retracing the same route we had
taken on the way in, but now everything had
changed. The villages were deserted, the fields
empty. The people we passed on the trail hurried
along, fear in their eyes. More MIGs barreled by
overhead, and once or twice we heard the distant
whop-whopping of helicopters, the most sinister
sound in the world if you have lived through a
chopper war on the wrong side.

It took us the remainder of the day and well
into the night to reach Morro; I don't know how I
ever made it. The afternoon heat was devastat-
ing—no matter how much water I gulped from
fetid pools and muddy streams, my throat felt like
cracked parchment. My feet, which had nearly
healed at Speena Bora, ripped apart again. By

dusk, as we made our way up the steep, boulder-choked head of the valley, I was literally crawling on my hands and knees.

As darkness fell, we reached the high ridge leading to Morro. The Afghans put me on one of the horses for the final stretch. As I rode, my mind's eye swarmed with hallucinations: stands of stunted timber became tunnels leading all the way to Peshawar, and rocks became houses, English country cottages with old friends holding out their arms beside glowing doors that turned at the last moment into patches of starlit rock. When we finally reached Morro, the sentries nearly shot us; they were expecting an attack from down the valley at any moment.

We spent the night in a tent a few meters across the imaginary borderline in Pakistan; I was so numb from it all, so brain dead, that I thought it was all over, that we were safe.

The next morning, the illusion was shattered. First, the mujahedin told us that the Zakhakhels had joined the battle on the Soviet side; only a large, well-armed party could cross the Tirah now. Were any resistance fighters headed that way from Morro? Foolish hope: with the Shurovee about to attack, every man would stay to fight. We had made it all the way to the frontier, but now we were trapped again. And then the bombing began, close by. Grazda and I crouched in the rocks with our two escorts as MIGs whizzed across the skyline, and high explosive grumbled.

Then the old peglegged commander summoned us. He had contacted the mujahedin down another valley by radio, and discovered that a large party of guerrillas were bound from there back to Pakistan; we could cross the Tirah with them. We left a few minutes later, accompanied by two of the youngest mujahedin I had ever seen—gawky, rosy-cheeked schoolkids with Kalashnikovs.

It was another nightmare day like the last, but even worse, a rerun of the same fear, fatigue, anguish, only now we were traveling straight toward the advancing enemy. My feet squelched in their own blood, blazing with pain.

I had thought the muj we were supposed to meet were close by, near Morro, but no; we tramped for hours and hours, farther and farther down the valley toward the plains. For a while, we passed bands of grim-looking retreating guerrillas, a depressing sight; then the gorge was empty, which was worse: a minatory emptiness, a bare stage set for tragedy, a tragedy starring us. And a *bad* tragedy, too, a story for snickers and smirks, like the Australian cameraman crushed by the runaway tank: *Did you hear about the two fools who walked right into the Spetsnaz camp? They say the Russians were laughing so hard they could barely shoot them.*

As the afternoon shadows lengthened, we came upon three white-bearded ancients, driving their flocks of sheep and goats. They told us the Shurovee were sweeping across the countryside below, killing everybody, destroying everything in their path. "And if they find you, they will surely kill you! By God, they are like animals— No, animals are good. They are children of the Devil!" There were tears in their eyes, as they begged us to come with them and hide in the mountains. But there was no turning back, and no place to hide.

It was evening when we finally reached the village where we were supposed to meet the party of guerrillas bound for Pakistan. By this time we expected disaster, and of course we got it. They were not there, and no one had any idea where they were. Almost all the villagers were gone, scattered into the hills and canyons. A few lightly armed mujahedin were preparing to defend the place.

We were sitting beneath a grove of trees in the square, wondering what to do, when suddenly we heard artillery fire, incoming. Huge columns of smoke rose from the mountain to the northwest. Then we heard small-arms fire, much closer. We sat there, frozen. A few moments later, a group of villagers came around the corner, carrying a dying man. He had just been shot by Soviet soldiers, on the outskirts of town. The man's wife wailed with grief, a high, thin, broken sound . . . And then we were running again, out of the village, back up the trail toward Morro. Our mujahedin escorts were gone; they had stayed behind to fight. The four of us went on, Ed and I and the two faithful farmers, unarmed, defenseless.

As darkness fell, we found ourselves sharing the trail with hundreds of civilians—peasants and their families—trying to escape the enemy offensive, driven from their ancient homes. It could have been Tibet, Guatemala, Ethiopia, Kurdistan, any one of the countless age-old nations twentieth-century industrial man has elected to destroy for no real bloody reason. To Orwell, the symbol of our time was a jackboot kicking in a human face, forever. To me, after Afghanistan, it was a bombed and blasted village, its people streaming away across a ruined landscape, and a refugee camp at the dead-end of the line. How could you not feel shame and disgust, at our century, its mindless cruelty, its worship of machinery, ideology, and money over the human heart and soul?

■ ■ ■

There was another side canyon leading east, up toward the Pakistani border. People said there was another marcaz at the summit, where we would be safe.

We climbed in near silence, in the darkness. Only the sounds of labored breathing, the scuffle of feet on earth and stone, mothers shushing their children with gentle whispers. We neared the crest of the mountain. Then, suddenly, the people ahead of us were turning back. There were Shurovee less than a hundred meters beyond, they whispered. Commandos, moving on the marcaz; they must have landed by helicopter or parachute earlier. Luckily, they hadn't seen or heard us; or else they weren't interested, they were set on their other prey. We turned again, tripping and stumbling down the steep trail.

Halfway down the mountain, one of our guides beckoned for us to stop. He drew us to one side, off the trail, pulled me close and whispered into my ear. Though he spoke Pushtu, the colloquial dialect of the mountains, I understood him perfectly.

"We can't go back to Morro," he said. "The refugees say the Shurovee have captured the marcaz. And we can't go back down the valley, the enemy are there, too. We must cross over into the Tirah; but if the people there find you, they will kill us all."

■   ■   ■

An hour later, as we trudged out across the fields of the Tirah Valley, the horizon behind us suddenly flared with a ghastly light. The flashes went on and on, like chain lightning, so bright that we could see our shadows, hard-edged and black as ink, in the trail. Rockets, artillery, air strikes, who knows? Strangely, there was no sound: just the pulsing flames, reaching to the top of the sky. The marcaz on the mountain, where we had been, was being systematically wiped out. The mujahedin couldn't have had a chance.

One of the farmers turned to us. "The Russian moon," he said in Pushtu. His tone was unmistakably disparaging. This homicidal glow was the Shurovee's version of moonlight, a contemptible perversion. Real moonlight belonged to the Afghans, the poor, the Faithful, the people of God and earth. No one and nothing could change that.

Around three A.M., we collapsed by the trail. Even the Afghans were weary, and besides, there was no way we were going to make it across the Tirah before daybreak. We wrapped ourselves in our thin blankets and huddled against the cold. We are going to die, I thought. In the morning the Zakhakhels will find us here, and kill us. I wondered if we would be shot, or beaten to death, or stabbed . . . I couldn't stop my thoughts. Fear drove them on until at last sheer fatigue dragged me under, into uneasy slumber.

Once or twice during the night, I was
awakened by prowlers, Zakhakhels. They left the
trail to look us over.

"Only Afghans," I heard them say. "Refugees
from the fighting." I pulled my head deeper under
the blanket.

I cowered there, praying the usual prayers of
those facing death and not able to face it; wartime
prayers. "Get me out of this, God, and I'll do
anything you want. If you just let me live, I'll do
anything, anything."

Then I was awake again; I saw the gray light of
dawn through a crack in the blanket, and there
was a growing clamor, the sound of many men and
horses approaching. Suddenly, I heard one of the
farmers shout, a joyful cry: "*Salaam aleikum!*" I
heard his friend laugh and call out a good-
humored jibe, something like "What kind of mujahedin are these, who don't even know where
they are?"

I threw off my blanket, and there in the trail
was a mob of Afghans, a string of packhorses. The
men bristled with weapons, and they were grinning at Ed and me. "We looked for you last
night," one of the farmers said, laughing, "but
you were lost!" I realized suddenly that these were
the guerrillas the commander from Morro had
contacted on the radio, the ones we were supposed to travel with. In the chaos of night and

battle they had missed the rendezvous at the village; then they had spent several hours searching for us fruitlessly along the border, skirmishing with Soviet troops repeatedly in the process. Finally, they decided to cross over into the Tirah and continue on to the Khyber Pass, hoping to run into us somewhere along the trail. And now they had. I couldn't believe it, and neither, I think, could they.

It took us most of the rest of that day to reach our goal, the town of Landi Kotal on the main road across the Khyber Pass to Peshawar. Another forced march, nothing to eat or drink, no stopping to rest . . . No one wanted to linger—the entire Tirah was a hostile armed camp now—and no one wanted to spend the night in those ghastly mountains beyond. By the time we arrived at Landi, in the early afternoon, my feet had been flayed, only a few patches of skin left, and I was sunstruck into a near coma. If I had tried to walk another half mile, another hundred meters, I'm not sure if I could have done it. An hour later, Grazda and I were speeding down off the Khyber in a muj jeep. They dropped us off on the Khyber road, in the honking, jostling traffic. It was Easter Sunday.

Over the next few days, reports filtered down to Peshawar about the fighting. The Shurovee had overrun everything, Speena Bora, Morro, the Achin and Nazian valleys, everything from Jalalabad to the Tirah. Scores of mujahedin had been killed, among them the old one-legged commander at Morro, and many civilians. The Soviets had destroyed large stocks of arms, ammunition, food, and medicine in the captured guerrilla camps.

But in the end, the Soviets had been driven back. The mujahedin regrouped behind them, threatening their supply lines up the winding valleys. At least twenty tanks were lost to mines and rocket-propelled grenades, and four aircraft were shot down. The Soviets retreated down from the mountains, and the holy warriors retook the heights, the vital passes; nothing had been won, nothing held.

The Shurovee, I realized, were not going to win this war. The mujahedin would always be there, no matter what happened. Part of it was the new weapons the mujahedin were receiving from the United States and China, of course: BM-1 and BM-12 rocket launchers, Stinger shoulder-fired antiaircraft missiles, Oerlikon guns . . . But even without the machinery, the Afghans would have prevailed in the end. The Hilltop Boys had known, in their own, crazy way: *Allaho akbar.*

twelve

As 1988 begins, the war definitely seems to be going the mujahedin's way. It is possible to dream of happy endings, peace with justice, honor. The Soviets are talking of pulling out for good, once and for all; the muj talk of a new regime in Kabul, Islamic, democratic, socially just. And old Professor Majrooh in Peshawar talks of teaching again. He is weary of politics and war, and this new Afghanistan will need knowledge, ideas, more than anything else. He smiles wistfully, musing of Hegel and Wittgenstein, classroom dialectic and dialogue, the friendly realm of pure ideas . . .

It is winter again, and I travel with a *Time* photographer, up through Terri Mangal to the Soviet/Afghan Army base at Jaji, where the muj are tightening their siege. It seems like a good place to document the turn in the war's fortunes.

We accompany a small group of guerrillas: two or three of Anwar's men from Jegdeleg (they are fighting on this front too, now), and a half-

dozen local partisans from a base camp in a
ruined village a couple of miles from the enemy
lines. To get to the village, we have to cross a
minefield in full view of the artillery gunners at
Jaji. We follow a narrow, winding path marked by
stones, keeping at least twenty yards between us;
a tighter group presents a more tempting target,
and this way, if anyone steps on a mine, there will
be no collateral casualties.

The village is a gloomy place, its tall adobe
buildings blown apart and shot full of holes, the
whole scene doused in heavy snow. We spend an
uncomfortable night with the muj in a basement
bunker, and the next morning, at dawn, we set out
for a raid on Jaji's outlying positions. It is snowing
again as we reach the muj forward line, a row of
foxholes and dugouts behind a low berm. Less
than a hundred yards away, across another minefield, we can see enemy fortifications and lagered
tanks. The barrel of the nearest T-62 is pointed
directly toward us.

The raid begins with the firing of our single-
shot Chinese BM-1 rocket launcher. The muj
stand up on the berm and hammer away with their
Kalashnikovs, and I stand with them, filming with
a video camera. So far so good, but only for a few
moments. Almost immediately things fall apart.
The enemy counterfire is withering: heavy
machine-gun shells and assault rifle bullets whiz,
whir, and hiss all around us. We duck down, and
keep firing, keep filming. Then a shout comes

from the BM-1 position below: the launcher has jammed. I can actually *feel* the bullets now, they are so close, deadly currents of air swishing against my skin. I dive in the snow, and then we are running, crawling for the nearest hole. An explosion, an airburst: a cannon shell has exploded thirty feet behind us, and a piece of shrapnel, luckily spent, whacks one of the muj in the head. And then we are in the comparative safety of the dugout.

A few minutes later, one of the mujahedin from Jegdeleg, a round-faced, ingenuous kid named Chinaur, whom I have known for years, goes out with an RPG to take a shot at the enemy. He fires once, prepares another round . . . And suddenly we hear a burst of machine-gun fire from the other side, a second rocket-propelled grenade round exploding, and someone shouts, "Chinaur's been hit!" We scramble from the hole, through the snow, and meet two guerrillas, dragging Chinaur to safety. They have already knotted a crude bandage around his head. He was hit by a DshK round, a ricochet, just as he squeezed the trigger on the grenade launcher. As he toppled over backward, he fired the projectile straight up into the air; luckily it went off somewhere out beyond the berm, in the minefields.

Chinaur doesn't look good: dark blood dribbles from his head, and he is semiconscious. While two of the local guerrillas run back to the rear to fetch horses, we begin half dragging, half carrying Chinaur away from the fighting. He appears to be going into hypothermic shock: he shivers violently, convulses, calls out deliriously for his mother. After a quarter of a mile or so we stop by the trail and build a fire, to try and warm him; the blizzard quickly blows it out. I lie against him, trying to shelter him from the whipsaw wind. At last the mujahedin return with horses, and we load him on board.

It is nightfall before two of Anwar's trucks, summoned by radio, make it from the border across the minefield to the village. The journey back is wild: we skid through the mined area on the snowy, icy track, headlights off to sneak past the gunners at Jaji. By some miracle, we make it through. It is snowing again when we reach the ridge above Terri Mangal. The truck bearing Chinaur speeds down the switchbacks into Pakistan, bound for the Kuwaiti Red Crescent hospital in Parachinar.

Back in Peshawar, we learn that the machine-gun slug didn't glance off Chinaur's head. It entered through his ear, and then traveled beneath the skull to the top of his brain. It took the Kuwaiti surgeons nine hours to remove it. But it looks as though he will live.

Two nights later, I am sitting in the lounge at "CBS House" in University Town, where I have rented a room. A car screeches to a halt outside, and a journalist I know comes crashing in the door. "Majrooh's been shot," he says.

"What?" I scramble to my feet, as if there is something I can do, if I just move quickly enough.

"Just now. At his office."

"Is he . . . ?"

He nods, coughs, rubs at his eyes, turns away. Like most of us on the Afghanistan circuit, he has become close friends with the leonine, eccentric old scholar. "Jesus, man," he says, "he took a full clip from a Kalashnikov from three feet away. There's blood all over the fucking door. The guy must have rung the bell at the gate, and when Majrooh answered it he just blew him away."

"Does anyone know who did it?"

"No. There was a car waiting. The guy escaped."

thirteen

No one was going to come out of this unscathed, unmarked; we were all going to get it in the end, dead, wounded or damaged in the soul, our love and laughter invisibly poisoned forever. There would be no clean hands, no pure hearts, when it was over . . . if it was ever over.

I returned to Peshawar a few months later to find that Anwar was on his way back to Jegdeleg, to make yet another attack on the Kabul-Jalalabad highway. I agreed to go along, of course—for no good reason; I was running out of reasons, though it didn't matter. The war had become like a fever inside me. I thought of the Plains Indians of the American West, the Dakota, Cheyenne, and the rest, how they cleansed their warriors with special rites when they returned from battle, win or lose, recognizing the curse that comes from making war. They were right, of course, but there was no one waiting to dance and pray the poison out of me. I was strictly on my own.

The omens were bad from the word *go* this time, big omens, small omens, all of them bent out of shape. When I met Anwar in Peshawar, he had changed. There was a different cast to his features, a warlord look, weary, heavy, sad, and brutalized. He didn't look like the same man, the high-spirited gentle idealist I had met back in 1984, and of course he wasn't: he too had seen too much, lost too much.

The preparations for the trip were a mess, even by muj standards. I was supposed to ride from Peshawar through the Tribal Area to the border in Anwar's jeep, but at the last minute it vanished to Islamabad on some vague errand. Ditto for the minivan he often used to ferry journalists. Anwar ended up arranging passage for me in a diesel truck loaded with Chinese rockets; I was supposed to crouch in a tiny crawl space behind the driver's seat to evade the guards at the Pakistani checkposts. Why hadn't the mujahedin paid off the Pakistanis, the way they always had before? Nobody knew. To top it all off, my translator disappeared when departure time rolled around, leaving me to travel on my own, and I was coming down with something, an evil combination of dizziness and nausea.

Except for the usual near-accidents and near-arrests, the trip through the Tribal Area went without incident. We stopped for the night at a guerrilla compound in Parachinar, and the next morning we pushed on to Terri Mangal. The weather had been hot on the way from Peshawar to Parachinar, but in Terri, at the base of the mountains, a chill wind blew and there were pockets of snow on the ground. Suddenly I found myself shivering through my Afghan clothes and my heavy Pakistani paratrooper's smock. At the same time, sweat was pouring off my forehead, scalding my eyes. I was definitely coming down with something. I remembered the long, grueling trip across the mountains from the border to Jegdeleg. Even though the mujahedin had built a road part of the way, so you didn't have to tramp the whole distance now, I began to wonder how I was going to make it. Every minute I felt worse and worse.

We muddled around Terri all day, one of those interminable, inexplicable delays that were standard operating procedure with the muj. The town hadn't changed much since my first visit in 1984. A mysterious explosion had virtually leveled the place a year or two before, killing hundreds—some blamed a Soviet rocket, others sabotage or an accident in the guerrilla arms dumps dug in under the town—but Terri had risen again in its old, undaunted image. There were the same stalls selling hand grenades and hashish, the same mobs of refugees, guerrillas, free-lance bandits, smugglers, and spies, the same battered ambulances and gaudy buses, the same smoking teahouses and slabs of bloody butcher's meat hanging on hooks, the same im-

mense ricks of logs, plundered from the mountains of Afghanistan.

At the western end of town, a new business
had opened: an adobe hut, with an enormous,
crude scale set up out front, presided over by a
burly Pakistani in a shabby skullcap. Caravans
came down the mountain, loaded with the destroyed and spent weapons of the Red army,
scavenged from a thousand battlefields: unexploded rockets; the husks of dud bombs; brass
artillery shells; the splintered carapaces of armored personnel carriers; the scorched, precious
bones of MIGs, Sukhois, Antonovs, gunships,
MI-8s. The caravanners unloaded their beasts,
the merchant weighed the slabs of metal debris,
and, after much haggling, he paid the laughing
Afghans: the dreams of an empire, sold off for a
few ragged banknotes by nomads and vagabonds.

There was a certain beautiful appropriateness
to that part of it all, of course—the stuff of the
oldest legends, the trickster who steals the tyrant
wizard's fire, the evil king toppled by innocents,
children—but at the same time, the whole scene
at Terri Mangal struck me with a kind of hopeless-
ness, a sense of despair. The logs from the mountains were giants; there had been mighty forests
up there, till the nomads cut them down to sell in
Pakistan. The nomads had turned to logging when
Soviet helicopters and jets slaughtered their herds
early in the war. Now the grand old forests, where
(the Afghans swore) tigers roamed within the

memories of living men, were going, going, gone
forever. Refugees still streamed down the pass
from the war zone—families, the survivors of
whole slain villages, plodding through the dust,
mud, and snow, people with lost, wounded eyes.
The empire had been defeated, turned to scrap,
the wreckage sold, but who had won?

Squatting there against a wall in the compound of the mujahedin arms depot, I looked at
Terri Mangal and I saw the end of the line,
extinction, extermination. Terminal City: the perfect spiritual capital for our time. Whichever way
you were headed, passing through Terri, you
weren't going anywhere good: or so it seemed to
me, as the fever began to roar in my ears, and I
thought of Jegdeleg and what awaited me there,
and I despaired. I wished I were somewhere,
anywhere, else—someplace safe, happy, peaceful, but I couldn't imagine where on earth that
might be.

The journey, of course, kept on falling apart.
Eventually, as evening fell, I rode on up the icy
track to the border. After a layover at Anwar's
base camp beyond the pass, I joined the hundreds
of mujahedin heading to Jegdeleg for the battle. A
ride in the back of a jampacked pickup truck took
me to Azrow and another nightfall. I arrived in the
middle of a brawl between two groups of guerrillas, and in the confusion I promptly fell into the

icy river that ran through the edge of the ruined
town. I clambered to the opposite shore and collapsed on the stony ground as the feuding muj
grappled with each other, screeching insults and
threats. I heard dozens of Kalashnikovs clicking
to full auto as men leveled their weapons. It was
an absolute nightmare, but I was too weary, too
sick to care. Eventually the furor died down and
someone led me inside, into a smoky, crowded
room where I fell asleep slumped against the wall.

The next morning, before dawn, I set out on
foot for Jegdeleg. Somehow, I had ended up with a
half-dozen muj I had never met before; I had no
idea who they were, but we were traveling together, either by accident or someone's design. I
really didn't care, I felt so bad.

The sun rose, and it turned into a blast fur-
nace of a day. I was feeling truly hellish now,
cramps convulsing my legs, twisting the muscles
till my bones felt like they were going to crack.
The fever had risen till it pushed me to the mar-
gins of delirium, and the landscape wobbled in
my eyes like an ugly mirage, a quaking mist of
sere rocks and earth, stunted trees, dry gulches.

We were crossing the same tract of badlands
Mister Etibari and I had traversed back in 1984.
It seemed like ten thousand years ago, and I felt
as if I had traveled those years on my hands and
knees, pushing an enormous slab of sorrow. *How
do you like your Holy War now?* a voice inside
asked. The sickness was turning my thoughts,

bending and breaking them, turning them against me. The dust in the trail sucked at my feet, pulling me down, pulling me back.

My companions could see how sick I was, but there wasn't much they could do. They insisted on carrying my pack for me; when they saw I was about to stumble to a halt, which happened more and more frequently, they would smooth out a piece of ground in the pallid shade of a rock and beckon for me to sit there.

"Everything be all right when we reach Jegdeleg," they kept saying, trying to encourage me. "Jegdeleg, no problem." I felt myself failing, and I hated myself for it.

We had crossed the last high pass on the trail, crossed a greenish valley; it was late afternoon. We were climbing yet another range of sullen hills, when suddenly something gave way inside me. My knees folded and I toppled over in the trail. I managed to scramble to my knees, but then I crumpled again. There was nothing I could do about it; I was finished.

The mujahedin gathered around me, and there was a worried conference that went on for several minutes. Finally, they decided to take me to a village nearby, a quarter of a mile or so off the main trail, where they thought they had some friends. They would leave me there for a few days,

long enough for me to recover and regain my
strength; then Anwar would send someone down
from Jegdeleg for me.

The way to the village led through a narrow cleft
in the mountain, hundreds of feet deep and only a
few paces wide at the bottom, a labyrinth of
grottoes and pools. We emerged into a narrow
valley, low stone walls, fields, clumps of trees
and bomb-damaged houses.

One of my companions gestured. "This
Yaghiband," he said. "Yaghiband village."

It was evening, time for prayers. Before we
entered the village, my companions knelt, facing
Mecca. I sat down on a crumbled wall and waited.
Suddenly something roared past my head, and
there was a tremendous explosion on the mountain just beyond us. My friends kept on praying,
imperturbable. I heard a distant peal of laughter,
and when I looked at the nearest cluster of
houses, on a knoll a hundred yards away, I saw a
lone mujahed dancing in triumph on a rooftop. He
was brandishing an RPG-7 grenade launcher
above his head.

He had fired a rocket at us—as a welcoming
salute, a threat, a joke, all three, who knows? If
his aim had been the least bit untrue, we would
have been killed or horribly injured. I looked
down at my companions. They didn't seem upset;

they were chuckling to each other, grinning as they completed their prayers.

On the way into the village, one of them turned to me and said, "Yaghiband man, all crazy-man. All, all crazy." He spoke with a tone of wholehearted admiration.

fourteen

I spent the next week in Yaghiband, trying to keep from dying.

It soon became clear that I had dengue fever, sometimes called breakbone fever for its agonizing pain. The fever rose and fell, and soared again, and I floated in and out of a haze of unknowing and uncaring, unable to move.

The illness was a kind of a madness in and of itself, and then there was Yaghiband. Since the local Jihad was in temporary abeyance, no enemy convoys, no bombing, the villagers of Yaghiband had evidently elected to fight a little war of their own, for no apparent reason. When I asked them why, they laughed, and shrugged, and laughed some more. There were five or six separate bands of muj, each holed up in its own set of ruins, and they sniped and potshot at each other whenever the mood struck them, which was almost always, from sunrise to sunset.

They didn't seem to be seriously trying to kill one another, but it was hard to be sure. One afternoon, the cook at the marcaz where I was staying went down to the river to get water. A few minutes later I heard a heavy machine gun, a 12.7 mm, hammering away, and I looked over the wall and saw the cook racing back across the fields, water flying from his buckets. Machine-gun slugs were kicking up puffs of dust all around his feet. The poor man ran faster and faster, finally jettisoning his pails and diving over the wall, landing next to me. He was gasping for breath, cursing and laughing, all at the same time.

One morning, while I was trying to rouse myself from another dreadful night of cramps, chills, and bad dreams, Rahmatullah and Ali came to see me. They were best friends, insepara-ble. Today they loitered in the doorway, blushing and giggling together like a couple of truant schoolboys. Finally Rahmatullah got up his nerve and stepped forward. "You have a-spi-reen?" he asked.

I reached for my pack, dug around in it, and found the stuffsack with the aspirin and water-purification tablets. As I got a couple of tablets for him, I asked him why he needed them; he told me he had been shot through the foot by an AK-47 two weeks before.

"Fighting the Shurovee?" I asked, and at this the two muj collapsed, whooping, holding on to each other to keep from falling down. They man-aged to tell me this story. Rahmatullah had been teasing Ali about his lack of a proper beard, as the latter had only a few sparse hairs on his chin. Ali slapped his friend, Rahmatullah slapped him back, and then Ali tried to tear his friend's beard out by the roots. "So I began to beat him," Rahmatullah laughed, pantomiming a beating. The two men were nearly speechless with mirth by now.

"So I," Ali said, "I took my Kalashnikov off the wall"—another pantomime—"and I shot him in the foot!" That was the punch line, and the two friends fell to the floor, clutching each other, howling. I couldn't help laughing, too. In my fever-stricken state, these demented little wars seemed to make sense: an eye for an eye and a foot for a beard. If someone bothered you, give him the gun. Why not?

The men of Yaghiband were good men, despite it all. Each night, they gathered in the room where I lay and they sang and danced for hours, trying to charm the fever out of me. Fists banged oil-can drums, and songs were sung, of love and war, triumph and tragedy. Bare feet stamped hard on the earthen floor.

As the nights wore on, the performances grew more manic, frenetic, till they teetered on the edge of absolute anarchy. The drumming crashed like thunder, and the dancers twirled and flung themselves out of this world, till they were totally

somewhere else, oblivion, you could see it in their
eyes. You felt that if you touched them you would
be electrocuted.

Finally, I felt strong enough to try for the border. I
had given up on Jegdeleg by now; I was still far
too ill to face the fighting there, on top of the long
journey back. I asked my friends at Yaghiband to
help find a horse and guide to take me back to
Azrow. It took a day or two, but they finally
arranged it. The horseman, a stranger from the
south, insisted on an exorbitant price, despite the
mujahedin's angry protests.

Was he really who and what I thought he was?
Or was it the fever, or funk, or simply that I just
didn't care anymore? But this is how I remember
it. The horseman was one of the most evil human
beings I have ever seen. Afghans wear their souls
on their faces, and this man's narrow raven's face,
with its stupid, hungry eyes, radiated malice and
treachery.

"He is bad man," one of the Yaghiband mujahedin whispered to me as I prepared to go. "But
he is only man with horse going to Azrow." And
then he added, "You be careful. You no trust.
And God be with you." Was this really how it
went down?

We left Yaghiband by a different route, following
a lonely rolling ridgeline where there were no

other travelers. I rode, carrying my pack on my back, and then walked to spare the horse, then rode again, and the whole time the horseman eyed me and my rucksack with a cold, famished gaze.

There was no time for omens or signs now, all of that was past. When I spied the glint of a knife concealed beneath his loose shirt, I knelt and picked up a rock from the trail, the size of a big man's fist, and I showed it to him. He looked at it, and then at me, and then he smiled malevolently, baring his long teeth. I could read his smile as if it were written in fiery red letters: "Maybe I will kill you," it said, "and maybe you will stop me. We shall see." I kept the rock in my hand as we traveled south, toward Azrow.

By the time we rejoined the main trail, the Soviets were bombing a few miles up the valley to the west: MIG-27s, with their ghastly ventriloquistic engines that always sounded as if they were everywhere, all around you, close enough to touch. The trail was crowded with mujahedin and civilians, hurrying, fearful. A woman passed me, panic in her eyes; she could have been Munch's model for *The Scream*.

I felt a mixture of terror and rage: people harried and hunted through their own homeland, death waiting to pop up from behind every ridge and rock pile. The fact that I was traveling with a man I couldn't trust, whom I had to watch and fear, seemed the last, intolerable straw. We half walked, half ran toward the pass, leading the useless, panicked horse, and I hefted the stone in my hand, and thought of smashing it into the horseman's skull, two inches above his ear . . . I wanted to smash him, and the whole evil scene, to pieces.

We had crossed the pass and were about four hours from Azrow when the trouble finally came. I wanted to keep going—I didn't want to travel at night with this man—but he insisted on stopping at a teahouse, a log lean-to in the bleakest gully bottom. I went to get a drink of water, and when I returned he was rifling my rucksack; he had my tape recorder out and was trying to stuff it under his shirt. If he had been a good man and had asked me for it, I might have given it to him, but this was different. I grabbed it, and we scuffled. He was stronger than I was, but I was angrier, and I managed to wrest it away from him. We knelt there, facing each other, furious. To save his pride, he demanded another ten dollars worth of afghanis for the rest of the journey to Azrow. I paid him half, and told him he could have the remainder when we got there. He counted the notes, showing his teeth in a feral sneer. Things were ready to explode.

As we left the teahouse, the shadows were deepening on the bluffs, in the gulches. The horseman insisted on riding: I was too poor a rider for the steep and narrow trail, he said. I shouldered my rucksack, felt the stone with my fingers. He lagged behind on the trail, and then I heard him shout a curse. I turned in time to see him wheel and ride back the way we had come. I threw the rock in his direction, but he was already gone.

Never travel alone on the trail in Afghanistan, especially at night: that was one of the laws you lived by in the war. To Afghans, strangers in the night were either enemies or victims, danger or prey: either way, you killed them if you could.

It was at least three hours' hard walking to Azrow, and I had perhaps one and a half hours of fading daylight left. There were no friendly villages or teahouses along the way, nothing. Earlier, we had passed several parties of armed Wahabis, Moslem fundamentalists from the Sudan and the Gulf, on their way to some private Jihad of their own. These non-Afghan holy warriors generally detested Westerners like myself; there were stories of them beating foreign journalists and medics, even trying to kill them. If I ran into any Wahabi war parties in my weakened state I would be dead, I thought.

But sometimes in the war you found yourself doing things you never would have dreamed of being able to do anywhere else; sometimes it seemed that strange powers watched over you.

Groggy with fever, legs like water, fifty-five or
sixty pounds on my back, I began trotting up the
trail toward Azrow. The track climbed steep disintegrating rock piles, traversed rubble heaps;
zones of malicious dust grabbed me, one step up
and one step back, two steps up and three steps
sliding downward . . . And still I staggered,
swam, flailed onward.

Several times, I encountered bands of Wahabis on the trail; in one narrow place, over a
chasm, I had to inch past twenty or thirty of them,
hard-faced men, lugging AKs and carbines, dag-
gers and grenades. Instead of barring my way, or
harassing me, they greeted me with a strange and
careful gentleness: "*Salaam, salaam.*" "May your
way be easy." "Go with God, brother." They
smiled upon me like so many angels.

The sun had sunk behind the peaks of the western
Safed Koh, and I was navigating in the dimmest of
twilights, picking my way through a jumble of
dark rocks, when suddenly I realized I was on the
mountainside overlooking Azrow.

I started trying to run down the last switchbacks to the village, where lanterns glowed and
wood smoke rose. I kept falling in the trail—not
tripping, just pitching over like a marionette
whose strings are cut. I wondered if I was going to
have to crawl the last two hundred yards, pushing

my pack before me like a dung beetle with his ball of treasure. God, I was tired.

Suddenly, a tall shadow rose up before me and took my hand. A golden light shone, and I was looking into the face of a man I had met before, one of the village elders. I must have looked awful, an apparition of disease and doom. He looked into my eyes and shook his head sadly, and led me the last hundred paces into the village.

Now I found myself in the room of a young commander whom I had met years ago on my way through, and who spoke fair English. Propped on cushions against the wall, I was drinking tea, and he was asking me to tell him what had happened, why I had returned at night, alone. I didn't understand exactly what he wanted, or why, but I told him of becoming ill on the trail, of the kind mujahedin at Yaghiband, and finally the horseman.

When I told of the horseman, something in the air changed, like a jump, a spark of static. But I was too tired and groggy to think clearly: ". . . I don't know . . . I guess he was trying to rob me . . ."

When I was finished, the young commander began asking me questions, quietly, as if satisfying some mild curiosity.

"You paid him to bring you on the horse to Azrow?"

"Yes."

"But he left you alone in the mountains?"

"Yes."

"And before, he tried to rob you?"

"But I stopped him."

There was a pause, as if he were still trying to fit things into place, things of great importance. I don't think I had any idea what was going on.

"You paid him to bring you here." Now it was less a question, more something he himself had to say.

"Yes." He was looking at me, as if he wanted me to say more. "Twice what the Yaghiband mujahedin said was right. Then more money at the *chai*-house."

"But he left you in the mountains."

"Yes."

He sat there, musing for a moment. There was no expression on his face I could give a name to.

Suddenly he rose, swung his blanket around his shoulders, went to the wall and unhooked his Kalashnikov from the nail where it hung. He took a clip from his camo vest, checked it, and snapped it into place. He looked over at me, not really focusing. "I will kill him," he said, and he went out the door.

I struggled to my feet and followed, shoes half on, half off. I found myself trying to say something

to change things. "Maybe just beat him," I said
feebly. But I didn't push the point as he turned to
face me. I looked at him, but I said nothing more.
I felt myself abandon the argument, and I felt him
acknowledge the fact.

"I will kill him," he said again. He paused.
"You are our friend. He left you alone in the
mountains. He tried to rob you." There was no
anger in his voice, just an immutable hardness.
He began walking again, toward the teahouses
and caravanserais at the far end of the ruined
town.

"But you don't know who he is." I spoke with
no conviction at all.

"I will find out," he said, and I knew he
would.

"But he rode the other way. He isn't here."

"He is here." I don't know why, but again, I
knew it was true. The horseman had come to
Azrow. Why? To die.

Suddenly, I was so tired I couldn't take another step, and anyway I just didn't care anymore.
The commander checked the clip on his AK-47
again, and flicked the safety off. He was walking
away from me, and there was nothing more to say
or do.

I leaned against the wall, and slid down till I
was sitting on the ground. I watched him go into
the first teahouse. He dangled his Kalashnikov
casually from one hand.

I knew what he would do: go from room to

room till he picked the horseman out, lure him outside with some friendly ruse, and then kill him. I imagined how it would all go down, and again, I didn't care. What did one more death matter, on top of a million or two others? And a bad death at that, a dishonorable man slain for nothing, in an age of murdered heroes and martyred saints?

In fact, I was glad. I felt as if this death was owed me: it was a matter of honor, vengeance, and the horseman knew the rules. Blood had to be spilled, to make things right again. Had it not been chosen? I had lived.

I sat against the wall, looking at the stars, waiting for the sound of the gun.

fifteen

989: This is supposed to be the climactic, the penultimate battle of the war. The Soviets have completed their withdrawal, and the Kabul regime totters as the mujahedin close in on the government-controlled cities and towns. Rumors say the CIA and the Pakistanis are pressuring the muj to finish the conflict quickly, no matter what the cost in casualties, but whoever or whatever is behind it, the mujahedin are preparing for an all-out assault on Jalalabad. When it falls, the rest of the Communist strongholds will tumble like tenpins, like dominoes . . . Or so the stories go.

I am working with Joe Gaal, a Canadian AP photographer. Joe and his wife, Kathy, who also covers the war, are two of the best friends I have ever had. I was with Joe a year ago, during the abortive muj attack on Asadabad, and I watched him run *toward* the exploding incoming artillery fire, cameras flailing, to get a good shot: like the best combat photographers, he is totally, mind-

lessly brave. He is also one of the funniest
characters I have ever met. Sample his tales of the
fake muj commander, call him Sharafat Nuristani, who conned Joe, Kathy, and an unfortunate
Japanese correspondent into hiring him as a guide
on a trip Inside several years back. The sleazy
Sharafat had gotten hold of a gallon jug of pre-
scription laxative from some foreign medical
group in Peshawar, and he insisted on drinking
from it constantly, thinking it was some kind of
farranji—a magic potion, elixir of health—with
predictable results. Sharafat had no idea of where
he was or what he was doing, and he eventually
got his three charges lost on a waterless mountainside and abandoned them there. The Japanese
journalist passed out from sunstroke and thirst,
and would have died if Joe hadn't stumbled on a
spring and dragged him there. When last heard
from, Sharafat was running a new racket in Peshawar, Swat, and Chitral, tricking recently arrived,
naive journalists into buying tickets on a supposed (and totally fictitious) mujahedin airline
flying into the Panjshir Valley. Joe can tell these
stories till you laugh so hard you hurt.

Along with an American doctor who is trying
to get to the war zone to train medics for the
upcoming offensive, Joe and I try and try to cross
the border into Afghanistan, but with no luck. For
some reason, the Pakistanis are trying to keep
journalists away from Jalalabad, and they have
the infiltration routes across the Khyber sealed up

tight as a drum. We try sneaking to the border, disguised as muj; we try getting permits from the Khyber Agency, to travel legally as far as Michni Point or Torkham, hoping to continue on covertly from there; we try pulling strings with friends in the Pakistani government, the press office, ISI. Nothing works. We get caught, busted, sent back, time after time.

After three weeks of futile effort, Joe and the doc head south to Baluchistan, to try to cross the border there. There is major fighting going on around Kandahar, too, and if they can't go to Jalalabad at least they hope to make it there.

Meanwhile, I decide to try Jalalabad one more time, and this time, wonder of wonders, I succeed. Be careful what you wish for, you might get it; be especially careful in war.

I travel in a van full of mujahedin. The only place we get stopped is at the Michni Point check-post, and the commander solves that by bribing the Pakistani official in charge. "Ten rupees," he laughs afterward; about eighty cents. Last month, he tells me, an Italian journalist paid eighteen thousand rupees, $1,500, to cross the border into Afghanistan. "But you are just a ten-rupee journalist!" Twenty minutes later we too have crossed the frontier. And two days later, I am on my way to the front, an hour farther to the west.

Something is wrong. The mujahedin are supposed to win this battle, but something is wrong. There

are no Stinger antiaircraft missiles, the muj have
run out, and the Americans were supposed to
replace them, but they haven't. In Pakistan, there
were rumors the attacking guerrillas would be
supplied with Hawk antiaircraft missile batteries
too, but there are no Hawks either. The mujahedin are wide open to air attack. And heavy
weapons are in short supply also. The commander
I am with spends a whole day negotiating the loan
of a captured truck-mounted BM-40 multitube
rocket launcher from another guerrilla group in a
nearby town, only to find there is no ammunition
for it. You can see a tragedy, a disaster, coming.

Still, the muj are brave, and they stream
toward Jalalabad to attack the enemy. I join them,
hitching west along the main road till I reach the
forward lines at Ghaziabad, just outside the city.
Ghaziabad was a tree farm before the war, and its
vast groves and concrete buildings provide some
shelter from the incessant air attacks. The MIGs
are everywhere, dropping cluster bombs. We take
cover in one of the battered, shrapnel-scarred
structures as explosions rock the earth outside,
and bomb fragments hammer the walls. The
assault on Jalalabad is being pounded to pieces.

The next day, back at the border, I watch as
dozens of ambulances, camouflaged with
branches and spattered mud, speed east toward
Pakistan, full of wounded. And then a pickup

truck pulls up and stops in front of the roadside
guerrilla base where I am staying. In the back are
fifteen or twenty men, very still. I think they are
sleeping, exhausted, till I notice the bullet and
shrapnel holes, the staring eyes, the stiff, twisted
limbs. These are just the commanders who were
killed today on the front northeast of the city.
Some of the guerrillas around me mutter angrily
that the Americans and Pakistanis planned it this
way, that they sent the mujahedin into battle
without proper weapons in order to kill them off.
The Pakistanis don't want a strong, independent
postwar Afghanistan, and the Americans fear another strong Islamic state in the region. It sounds
crazy, but everything out here is crazy. Who
knows? It could be true. And what do I say,
anyway? "I'm sorry"?

My camera breaks, and in my depression and
confusion I decide I will sneak back across the
border into Pakistan, get it fixed at Uncle Tony's
in the Peshawar bazaar, and then sneak back. Of
course, I am arrested as soon as I set foot in
Pakistan, by a bevy of bribe-seeking officials.
They are not pleased at all when they find I have
almost no money to baksheesh them with, and
only the chance arrival of Nadir Khan, a local
Pakistani tribal chief of my acquaintance, saves
me from jail or worse. Throughout most of the
years, Nadir Khan worked with the Soviets and

the Kabul regime against the mujahedin, in return for arms and cash; now he has switched over to the muj side, sensing advantage. Nadir Khan's Zakhakhel faction controls the liquor and gun-running action on the Khyber, and can put close to four thousand warriors in the field, armed with rocket launchers, antiaircraft missiles, cannons, and machine guns. Nobody wants to run afoul of him. When the bent officials see that Nadir Khan and I are friends, they tell me Go, go to Peshawar, and don't come back.

Over the next days, the battle of Jalalabad degenerates into an ugly, inconclusive quagmire, the stalemated slaughter of bombardment and trench warfare. I just don't have the heart or stomach for it at this point. The war should be over by now, not dragging on into new campaigns, offensives, fronts . . . nightmares forever and ever. I give up the story, decide to head back to the States.

In Islamabad, I stop off at the AP office to see Kathy. The night before I fly out, Joe calls from Quetta. He and the doctor have had a disastrous trip, too. Their muj driver got lost somewhere out on the plains south of Kandahar, and to try to make up time he drove ninety miles an hour through the nocturnal darkness across mine-strewn fields. At one point, they passed a truck exactly like theirs, burned out and gutted. The driver turned and smiled at them: *"They hit mine,"* he said, driving on faster than ever. Then they broke an axle while they were passing next to an enemy air base, and were stuck there way past dawn fixing it, while jets and helicopters took off and flew overhead. The next night, they came to a river swollen with spring floods. In front of them was a whole caravan of trucks and buses loaded with hundreds of people. As Joe and the doctor watched, the vehicles inched out into the swirling waters. Suddenly, a great flood wave surged down the channel, sweeping everyone and everything away; no one was saved.

The mujahedin had given up on reaching Kandahar then; they turned around and headed back to Pakistan. The whole trip lasted more than forty hours, nonstop. Joe is totally exhausted, done in, and my bad news from Jalalabad doesn't help. "I don't know how much more of this I can take," he tells me. "It just goes on and on, on and on, and it never stops."

sixteen

three months have gone by since I left Jalalabad: almost time to start planning another trip back. As usual, I have drifted through my stay in peacetime America in an uneasy, uncomfortable daze. I don't feel at home at home anymore; I don't feel at home anywhere. Lost in Limboland, lost everyplace I go.

Claire and I go camping out in Utah for a few days, in the canyon country. I feel comparatively good out there: there are few if any people, and the pale wind-polished cliffs, pure blue skies, and immaculate drifting sands call up daydreams of Afghanistan, a dream Afghanistan without the terror, the fury, the agony of war. When we return to Telluride, there are two messages from Kathy on the answering machine. She gives a number in Canada, and asks me to call back immediately. Her voice sounds hoarse, unsteady, but I put it down to travel fatigue—she must have just flown in from Pakistan—and the distortion of long distance. Or perhaps I have guessed that something is wrong, even what it is, and I want to block it out. At any rate, I don't return her call.

That evening, the phone rings; I answer it, and I hear Kathy on the other end. "Hello? Rob? Oh, Rob, I'm so sorry—but Joey's dead." I stand there, the phone against my head; I try to talk, to say the right things, as everything inside me shatters, blown to bits, blasted, a direct hit from a two-thousand-pound bomb straight through the heart.

Two days later, I get a postcard from Joe in the mail, written the same week he died:

Dear Rob: Now in a place a hell of a lot better than other ones I've spent time in over the last year . . . Appreciate your concern for me in your letter. Only others who have experienced it can really understand. My friend in Hong Kong said I was crazy after I tried to talk to him about it. Went to Jalalabad after I talked to you on the phone, was there during 2nd and 3rd attacks to capture city. Several hundred muj (part of the thousands) tried to overrun the airport from the side using conventional tactics of moving under an artillery barrage from trench to trench until they got to 150 meters of perimeter. Muj divided into squads of 25 to 30 men. I was with the commander's squad which led the assault. Got blown to pieces. Very heavy small arms, mortar, grenade and tank fire. Commander's brother and

a 15-year-old muj killed by direct hit from tank
shell. Commander critically wounded by same
shell. Trapped by heavy Gov't. fire in front and
mortars and bombing behind us. Muj providing
artillery support continuing shelling not realizing
how close we were. Rocket landed short, into a
group of muj near us—2 killed, 3 wounded. Out
of 25 of us, 17 got back without being hit. Trying
to forget everything, but it's tough. You realize
you have forgot how to relax. See you in
Peshawar.

Take care,
Joe

seventeen

A couple of months after Joe's death, Kathy and I take his ashes into Afghanistan, to Ghaziabad, and scatter them across a field of green meadowgrass and wildflowers. Bombs are exploding along a mountain spur to the northeast; more fighting, around the outskirts of Jalalabad. Forgotten by the rest of the world, the war goes on: no peace, no solution, no answer.

On the way back from Peshawar to Islamabad at dusk, in the AP bureau Mitsubishi, driving much, much too fast, we slam side-on into another car. He tried to cut across two lanes, panicked, and stalled. If it weren't for the seat belt I am wearing I would be dead, but as it is I am by far the worst hurt in either vehicle: two broken ribs, the rest on the right side ripped loose from the sternum, and something torn, wrenched in my back. Kathy has a lumpy cut on one elbow. I kick the bent door open and stagger out onto the debris and shattered glass in the roadway. I can barely

breathe; I feel totally screwed up. A perfect end-
ing to a perfect day: saying good-bye to a best
friend I will never see again, almost saying good-
bye to myself. It's so awful, it's hilarious.

Herat lies in ruins; according to travelers coming
from western Afghanistan, the whole far side of
the city is a flattened no-man's-land of gutted
blocks, trenchlines, minefields, and burned-out
vehicles, where militia groups, muj bands, and
banditos snipe and firefight over turf and burned-
out ideals. Soviet planes fly cross-border sorties
south to whack recalcitrant villages on the outskirts. The old, elegant, great-hearted city I knew
before the war is gone.

No one stops anymore at the hidden village
where Mister Etibari and I and our mujahed
friend took shelter from the storm back in the
winter of 1984, a lifetime ago. Before they pulled
out of Afghanistan the Shurovee landed copterborne commandos, lined up the villagers who had
been welcoming the mujahedin and their friends,
and machine-gunned them. The bandit king of the
Safed Koh and his white-bearded brother were
among those killed, they say. So many places you
can't return, even in your memories . . . Gone.

I keep going back; why, I don't really know.
Maybe you lose so much that you just can't give it

up: lost friends, dreams, innocence. You've invested too much blood in the vision. To forget would be a kind of dying, a death of the spirit, far worse than taking a lethal Kalashnikov round, a terminal blade of BM-40 shrapnel, in those wild, indomitable mountains. Nobody cares about Afghanistan anymore, but, believe me, it was the holiest of wars, and those hopelessly brave warriors I walked with, and their families, who suffered and endured so much for faith and freedom and who still are not free, they were truly the people of God.